Bitcoin

FOR

DUMMIES®

A Wiley Brand

Bitcoin
FOR DUMMIES®
A Wiley Brand

by Prypto

FOR DUMMIES®
A Wiley Brand

Bitcoin For Dummies®

Published by: **John Wiley & Sons, Inc.,** 111 River Street, Hoboken, NJ 07030-5774, www.wiley.com

Copyright © 2016 by John Wiley & Sons, Inc., Hoboken, New Jersey

Published simultaneously in Canada

For general information on our other products and services, please contact our Customer Care Department within the U.S. at 877-762-2974, outside the U.S. at 317-572-3993, or fax 317-572-4002. For technical support, please visit www.wiley.com/techsupport.

Wiley publishes in a variety of print and electronic formats and by print-on-demand. Some material included with standard print versions of this book may not be included in e-books or in print-on-demand. If this book refers to media such as a CD or DVD that is not included in the version you purchased, you may download this material at http://booksupport.wiley.com. For more information about Wiley products, visit www.wiley.com.

Library of Congress Control Number: 2016932286

ISBN 978-1-119-07613-1 (pbk); ISBN 978-1-119-07614-8 (ePub); ISBN 978-1-119-07641-4 (ePDF)

Manufactured in the United States of America

Contents at a Glance

Table of Contents

Introduction

Welcome to *Bitcoin For Dummies*! But just what is bitcoin? How can there be digital money? Is it, like, some kind of Internet money? Is it something you should even be concerned about, or indeed should you shy away from it? In the news, bitcoin coverage tends to be sketchy. You may have read articles about people losing their money, or using bitcoin for illicit purchases on the black market. Or you may have read amazing success stories of people and businesses flourishing by using it.

Fear not, dear readers. This book strips away the mystery and gets down to the facts. It patiently explains exactly what bitcoin is, discusses some of the possibilities this wonderfully disruptive yet inspirational technology holds, and lays out some of the potential benefits for all of us. Bitcoin could change our lives in a similar way that the Internet has done over the last few decades.

In short, this book tells you everything you need to know to get started. So what are you waiting for? Let's, um . . . get started!

About This Book

Bitcoin For Dummies tells you a bit about the history of this fascinating technology and explores bitcoin as a concept and product. We show you how to open a wallet so that you can safely store your own bitcoins. We even guide you through the process of obtaining some bitcoins. We demonstrate what you may do with those bitcoins and talk about the potential for earning money with them too. We touch upon regulatory and legal frameworks as they currently stand. We detail mining bitcoin and explain how you could become involved in that — and why it may not be worth it.

We also prop up the hood and take a good look underneath. We detail how transactions work within the bitcoin environment and delve deep into blockchain technology. We gaze into our crystal ball and speculate on how bitcoin and its blockchain system may develop in the future and how they may change many aspects of our lives. To round things off, we provide you with online resources to keep you up to date and help you become involved with the online community that is actively supporting bitcoin. Come on and join us. We think this will be one heck of a ride!

Foolish Assumptions

The only assumption we have about you, our reader, is that you are interested in learning some of the basics about this new form of currency. We hope you'll like what you read and will want to create your own wallet, start using bitcoin, and spread the word to friends and colleagues. But our basic assumption is that you've picked up this book because you want to find out more before jumping on board.

We also assume you have some basic experience with computers and the Internet. We figure you already know how to find your way around the Internet and how to take some simple steps to safeguard yourself online and protect your money. We don't expect you to be a tech expert who knows all there is to know about computing.

And that's because you don't need to be an expert to get started with bitcoin.

Icons Used in This Book

To help you pick out the information most useful to you, we've used a few graphical icons in the book to highlight key details. Whenever you see the following icons in the page margin, this is what you can expect from that paragraph:

We like to dispense our advice on a warm plate, ready for your consumption. This icon highlights our top tips for getting the best out of bitcoin and often includes insider knowledge to help you to achieve what you want as quickly and efficiently as possible.

When you see this icon on the page, we're speaking to you with our deep, velvety public information announcer voice: These are the most salient points to squirrel away in your brain for later use.

This icon warns you of common mistakes or pitfalls that could trip you up when it comes to bitcoin. We know you're going to use your common sense when it comes to money and online transactions, but from time to time we just like to tap you on the shoulder and say, "Pay attention and be careful." This icon is that tapping finger.

Online finances, the Internet, and bitcoin itself all have many weird and wonderfully specific ways of describing things, doing things, and generally flummoxing the unwise. Sometimes having a bit of slightly esoteric background knowledge helps, even if it's not directly related to getting the best from your bitcoin. This icon flags the parts you can safely skim over and not lose out by doing so.

Beyond the Book

But wait, there's more! We've not only put together a book that explores bitcoin, but we've also compiled some online bonus bits (at www.wiley.com/extras/bitcoin) to take things further:

✔ An online Part of Tens with tips on how bitcoin can help you.

✔ Two other online articles that cover certain aspects of bitcoin and banking, plus more about the blockchain.

✔ A handy e-cheat sheet (at www.dummies.com/cheatsheet/bitcoin) to keep important info handy at all times.

Where to Go from Here

As with all *For Dummies* books, you can start anywhere you like: Each chapter is designed to be as self-contained as possible. That said, we don't like to repeat ourselves too often, so you'll spot plenty of references to other chapters throughout.

If you're not sure where to begin and don't feel like engaging in the usual practice of "starting at the beginning," here are a couple suggestions:

✔ Chapter 9 is a great place to get started: Before you find out too much about bitcoin itself, this chapter will tell you whether bitcoin is used (and legal) in your country.

✔ If you want to plunge straight in and set up a bitcoin wallet, enabling you to acquire and spend bitcoin, flick through to Chapter 5.

✔ Chapter 10 is a good place for the level-headed to begin; it looks at bitcoin security, outlines the relative safety of using it, and suggests precautions you should consider taking.

✔ Chapter 12 provides you with some ready-made inspiration — it's all about what you can do with bitcoin once you have some. In other words, spend, spend, spend.

Having said that, you can certainly start at the very beginning . . . it's a pretty good place to start after all. Wherever you kick things off, we hope you enjoy and get something valuable from this book.

Part I
Bitcoin Basics

In this part . . .

✔ Get familiar with the basics of what bitcoin is, how it came to be, and how it works.

✔ Find out how to obtain your own bitcoins and where to keep them once you have them — and where not to.

✔ Check out the advantages and disadvantages of bitcoin as a currency and a technological system.

✔ Read all about mining, funding, trading, and earning bitcoin.

Chapter 1

Introducing Bitcoin

● ●

In This Chapter

▶ Getting to know a bit about bitcoin

▶ Understanding how bitcoin benefits us all

▶ Staying safe and stashing your cash

● ●

So, bitcoin . . . you know it's a new form of money — a *digital currency,* to be exact — but just how does it work? Sit yourself down comfortably, and we will begin with the basics, the three major aspects of bitcoin:

▸ **Origin:** How it came to be

▸ **Technology:** How it works behind the scenes

▸ **Currency:** Using bitcoins as money

Exploring each of these aspects will help you understand bitcoin (or BTC, as it's sometimes known) and find out whether and how it can help you. Don't worry — we will stay top-level for now. Later chapters dig deeper.

Ready? Let's go.

The Origin of Bitcoin

The most important aspect of bitcoin may be the concept behind it. Bitcoin was created by developer Satoshi Nakamoto. Rather than trying to design a completely new payment method to overthrow the way we all pay for things online, Satoshi saw certain problems with existing payment systems and wanted to address them.

The concept of bitcoin is rather simple to explain: During the financial crisis of 2008, people from all over the world felt its debilitating economic effects. And at the time of this writing (early 2016), many are still feeling the effects in terms of the dwindling value of their *fiat currency* (the currency approved by a country's government). As the global financial system teetered on the brink of collapse, many central banks engaged in *quantitative easing* — or in simple terms, turned on the printing presses. Central banks flooded the markets with liquidity and slashed interest rates to near zero in order to prevent a repeat of the Great Depression of the 1930s. The effect of this was large-scale fluctuations in fiat currencies and what has since been termed *currency wars* — a race to competitively devalue so that an economy can become more viable simply by its goods and services being cheaper than those of its neighbors and global competitors. The response of central banks around the world was the same as it always has been when these things happen: Governments had to bail out affected banks and they printed extra money, which further devalued the existing money supply.

In bailing out the banks, there was a net transfer of debt to the public purse, thus adding to future taxpayer liabilities. This created a sense of social injustice among some quarters. Aside from that, no one really knows what the long-term effects of quantitative easing will be. Perhaps inflation at some point in the future and a further devaluation of those fiat currencies who engaged in the schemes? What seemed clear is that central bankers, supposedly acting independent of governments, were taking many economies into the unknown and were prepared to devalue their fiat currencies at will just to keep the wheels turning. In doing so, they bailed out the very same institutions and bankers whose reckless behavior had brought about this crisis in the first place. The only other option would have been to let the whole system collapse and be purged, as for instance happened in Iceland. That country defaulted on its debt and endured great economic turmoil in the aftermath of that event.

Therein lies the genesis of bitcoin: a decentralized financial system taken out of the hands of a few elite global decision-makers.

Satoshi Nakamoto decided it was time for a new monetary system, one so different from the current financial infrastructure that you could even call it a disruptive force. Whether or not bitcoin was ever intended to completely replace the financial infrastructure remains unclear, but we do know that multiple banks are looking at the technology that powers bitcoin, because they see its potential and want to adopt this technological power for their own use. They are free to do so, of course, as the core bitcoin technology — known as a *blockchain* (much more on that in Chapter 7) — was open source from day one for everyone to see. Creating bitcoin as open source meant that anyone was allowed to come up with their own improvements and build platforms on top of it.

Viewed from this angle, bitcoin could be said to have a driving ideology. It is about so much more than just using the associated coin as a payment method. It is about using the underlying technology and discovering its full potential over time. How you decide to use that technology is completely up to you. It can be adapted to fit nearly any financial need you can imagine. All you really need to do is be open to the technology itself. Even though you may not grasp the entire concept from the start, just keep an open mind.

Let's face it: The intersection of finance and technology is plagued with troubles. All of us have been affected by the banking crises of the 21st century, and quite a few countries are still struggling to recover from that financial fiasco. Bitcoin developer Satoshi Nakamoto was a victim of this mismanagement by central banks and thought long and hard to come up with a proposed solution. The mainstream financial infrastructure is flawed, and a viable alternative is more than welcome. Whether or not that alternative will be bitcoin remains to be seen.

When Satoshi Nakamoto came up with the idea of bitcoin, one key factor was destined to play a major role: decentralization. Decentralization means we are all part of the bitcoin ecosystem, and we all contribute to it in our own ways. Rather than relying on a government, bank, or middleman, bitcoin belongs to everyone, in a system called *peer-to-peer,* and we all make up the bitcoin network. Without individual users, there is no bitcoin. The more people embrace bitcoin, the better it works. Bitcoin needs an ever-expanding community who actively use bitcoin as a payment method, either by buying goods and services with bitcoins or offering goods and services in exchange for bitcoins.

Due to the digital currency's free market spirit, anyone in the world can set up their own business and accept bitcoin payments in a matter of minutes. Plus, existing business owners can offer bitcoin as an alternative payment method, with the potential to expand their customer base on a global scale. It's easy to do your bit(coin) and get involved.

Getting Technical

As you'd expect with a peer-to-peer payment system, the technology powering bitcoin digital currency is a force to be reckoned with. A lot of focus is being put on making bitcoin's blockchain technology a powerful tool in the financial sector. That's only to be expected, because most of the focus regarding bitcoin revolves around the currency aspect.

Bitcoin's technology offers unprecedented technological options and abilities only dreamt of a few years ago. And a great deal of potential remains hidden below the surface for the time being, as some of the world's brightest minds try to grasp the potential implications of integrating bitcoin technology into our daily lives. There is more discussion about this in Chapter 3.

 Bitcoin technology has been underestimated in the past, and to be honest, it has a bit of a checkered history. Several platforms have been created in order to make bitcoin more accessible and usable, but that has not always lead to a happy ending — especially when it comes to security. New tools like bitcoin represent a learning curve for everyone. Bitcoin is only slowly starting to mature in that regard.

The potential of bitcoin technology has attracted many interested parties from all aspects of life. The frontrunners are people in the financial sector, who are intrigued by the *open ledger* aspect of bitcoin technology. Open ledger means anyone in the world can see every financial transaction on the network take place in real time. Even though that idea might seem a bit scary, open ledger in a system allowing us to track multiple things would be beneficial. None of these implementations have to be related to finance *per se*, but there are plenty of options worth exploring in that sector.

 When it comes to accepting bitcoin payments, there's a lot of room left to explore. Although integrating a bitcoin payment option onto your website just takes a few minutes, in-store payments are a slightly different manner. However, multiple payment processors will gladly help you convert your bitcoin transactions to local currency. To make that deal even better, you receive payments to your bank account the very next business day, rather than waiting up to a week for credit card payments to clear through the banking network. And the fees for accepting bitcoin as a payment solution are likely to be low as well.

Bitcoin as Currency

Whenever we talk to people about bitcoin, one of the first things they mention is the current bitcoin price. At the time of writing, the price hovers around $300 per bitcoin.

Bitcoin had nearly no value until 2011 and only then started climbing the charts slowly. However, in 2013 bitcoin saw a peak price of well above $1,100, which some attributed to market manipulation by a trading bot on the largest bitcoin exchange at that time.

The bitcoin price is determined by its users under the free market principle of supply and demand. And although the bitcoin supply is limited to 21 million "coins" in total — to be reached by 2140 — no huge demand exists for this digital currency just yet. As bitcoin matures further over the next few years, that story might change.

Why 21 million? Nobody knows. Some believe it's because it's a mathematical equation that brings us to the amount of coins available until the year 2140 with rewards being halved every four years.

Keep in mind that bitcoin is a *payment method* that can be used online and in the real world as well. However, that does not make bitcoin a *currency*, because it lacks certain aspects of the "ground rules" that determine whether a payment method is a currency or not. But according to most experts around the world, bitcoin is to be considered a *digital currency* in its truest form. As we try to wrap our hands around this new currency technology, who is to say whether or not that term is correct? What we can say is that bitcoin is a valid payment method for many goods and services, and that is what makes its digital aspect so much fun to explore.

By being a decentralized payment method (meaning no government or official entity controls it), bitcoin lets anyone in the world accept a digital currency payment from anyone else in the world. Bitcoin is the same digital currency across borders, no matter what the country's physical currency, and can be converted into nearly any local currency on request. With no transaction fees to speak of, and being able to receive your payments the next business day, what's not to like? On top of that, mobile payments are on the rise, so bitcoin is an excellent alternative mobile payment method to take your customer base to the next level, at very little cost.

Bitcoin as a currency tool

For bitcoin to be widely thought of as a currency, it needs to be used more and more. As you might imagine, it's hard enough to convince merchants to accept bitcoin as a brand new currency, but it is even harder to convince consumers to get involved with digital currency.

The advantages for the merchants are crystal clear: Bitcoin cuts down on fees and other costs. But if no one visiting your store is using bitcoin as a payment method, there is no benefit in accepting it either. So it's up to the consumer to set the wheels in motion.

To make bitcoin a more convenient currency tool, you can turn to familiar-looking plastic:

- ✔ Prepaid bitcoin cards
- ✔ Bitcoin debit cards

These plastic cards can be topped up with bitcoin — or linked to an existing bitcoin wallet (for more on wallets, see Chapter 5) — allowing you to spend digital currency wherever major credit cards are accepted. The merchant still pays the same fees as with regular card transactions and still receives funds in local currency.

Bitcoin is still some way from being a mainstream payment method; retailers need to be convinced to accept bitcoin. We think the time has come to start convincing the everyday consumer to leave the cash and cards at home and pay with bitcoin using their mobile device. That will not happen overnight, so until then, bitcoin users must be patient (while reveling in the thought that they're ahead of the game).

Bitcoin and retailers

As a forward-thinking retailer, you should be ready and prepared to accept bitcoin payments for your online or brick-and-mortar shop. Accepting bitcoin payments doesn't require you to deploy additional hardware, as it peacefully coexists next to your existing payment infrastructure. You do need an Internet connection however, but most retailers already have that.

Here are some of the main advantages of accepting bitcoin:

- ✔ Accepting bitcoin payments is subject to very low transaction fees — a welcome change from the 3 to 5 percent per transaction you lose when accepting any type of card transaction.

- ✔ Bitcoin payments can be converted to a local currency of your choice, and funds are deposited to your bank account the very next business day. If you're using a good payment processor, they will charge you only a small margin to convert the bitcoin to your local currency. Compare that to card transactions, where you have to wait up to a week or so before you receive the money — minus the 3 to 5 percent transaction fee plus an additional fee for any currency conversions — and bitcoin is the clear winner across the board.

- ✔ Bitcoin is a global currency. It works the same in every country around the world. Everywhere you go, the bitcoin symbol is the same.

✔ Bitcoin value is calculated to the eighth digit after the decimal point (the hundred millionth), unlike cash, which is only broken down to hundredths, or cents. For example, trading in U.S. dollars allows you to charge $11.99. Bitcoin would allow a charge of 11.98765432 BTC. Although this may not seem to be of significance now, should the value of BTC exponentially increase in the coming years, those additional decimal places will be very useful for accurate pricing in the future.

✔ Accepting bitcoin payments lets you expand your potential customer base on a global scale, as there is no need to offer a plethora of local currencies when offering bitcoin will suffice.

✔ Bitcoin-to-bitcoin means it keeps its value during the transaction and it is later on converted to a currency of your choice.

Bitcoin and consumers

As a consumer, the advantages of using bitcoin are pretty straightforward. First of all, you no longer need to use cash to pay for goods or services at a bricks-and-mortar location. Cash is clunky to use, and it fills up your wallet with banknotes and your pockets with coins so quickly that you just want to spend it faster to get rid of it (or is that just me?). Plus, the ever-present — if slight — chance exists that you may be carrying counterfeit money without even knowing it. Should you ever be in that situation while trying to pay for something, you will not be having a fun afternoon, we can tell you that much.

Bitcoin is also a viable alternative to paying for goods and services with your bank account or bank/credit/debit card, for the following reasons:

✔ Rather than relying on the services provided by a centralized service such as a bank, bitcoin lets you make any payment to anyone at any time, regardless of business hours, weekends, and holidays.

✔ When you make an online payment, it is processed immediately.

✔ Bitcoin is a borderless digital currency, operating in the same manner in Europe as it does in North America, Africa, Asia, Latin America, and Australia. Anyone in the world can use bitcoin to pay for anything else in the world, albeit you might have to jump through some hoops in order to get there.

✔ Many efforts are underway to push bitcoin's acceptance by merchants, combined with new and improving alternative ways to spend bitcoin conveniently (such as the previously mentioned debit cards).

Figuring Out How Bitcoin Works

Bitcoin is changing the way people think about money by planting a seed of doubt in people's minds — in a positive and thought-provoking way. Mind you, given the financial crises over the past decade, it's understandable that some people are trying to come up with new and creative solutions for a better economy. Bitcoin, with its transparency and decentralization, may prove to be a powerful tool in achieving that goal.

One thing bitcoin does is bypass the current financial system and could therefore potentially provide services to unbanked and underbanked nations all around the world. Whereas most people in the Western world find it normal to have a bank account, the story is quite different elsewhere. Some countries in Africa, for example, have an unbanked population of anywhere from 50 to 90 percent. Do these people have less right to open and own a bank account than Americans or Europeans do? Absolutely not, but doing so may come with rules so strict as to be unobtainable for many citizens.

For a while now, society has been evolving toward a cashless ecosystem: More and more people use bank and credit cards to pay for goods and services both online and offline, for example. Mobile payments — paying for stuff with your phone — are now on the rise, which may become a threat to card transactions. Bitcoin has been available on mobile device for years now.

We're slowly starting to grasp the concept of blockchain technology's potential and future uses: A blockchain (see Chapter 7) can do pretty much anything; you just have to find the right parts of the puzzles and fit them together.

Here are some examples of what bitcoin technology is capable of (see Chapter 3 for more on these):

- ✔ Taking on the *remittance market* (transfers of funds between two parties) and coming out on top in every aspect.
- ✔ Sending money from one end of the world to the other end in only a few seconds.
- ✔ Converting money to any local currency you desire.
- ✔ Overriding the need for a bank account, making bitcoin an incredibly powerful tool in unbanked and underbanked regions of the world.

What if you live in an unbanked region and have no reliable access to the Internet? There's a solution for that as well: Some services allow you to send text messages to any mobile phone number in the world in exchange for bitcoin or a few other digital currencies. Once again, bitcoin proves itself a very powerful tool in under-banked and unbanked regions of the world.

Perhaps the most impressive showcasing of what bitcoin can do is the bitcoin network itself. All transactions are logged and monitored in real time, giving users unprecedented access to financial data from all corners of the world. Furthermore, the blockchain lets you track payments' origins and destinations, even as money is on the move in real time. Such valuable insight will hopefully be adopted in the current financial infrastructure, even though there may be a period of adjustment while that takes place.

Using Bitcoin Anonymously

One of the biggest misconceptions surrounding bitcoin is whether or not digital currency is truly anonymous. The simple answer to that question is "no, not entirely." But a certain level of anonymity is tied to using bitcoin and digital currency in general. Whether you can label that as "anonymous enough" is a personal opinion.

Whenever you use bitcoin to move funds around, you can essentially hide your identity behind a bitcoin wallet address (Chapter 5 talks more about wallets). These wallet addresses are a complex string of numbers and letters (both lower- and uppercase) and provide no insight into who you are or where you're located. In that regard, bitcoin offers a certain level of protection you won't find in most other payment methods.

But that is also as far as the anonymity goes, because bitcoin wallet addresses are part of a public ledger — the *blockchain* — which tracks any incoming and outgoing transfers to and from any address at any given time. For example, if we were to send you 0.01 BTC right now, anyone in the world could see the transfer from wallet address A to wallet address B. No one would know whom those addresses belong to, but the transaction itself would be in plain sight.

Once someone knows your public wallet address, they can monitor it at the `www.blockchain.info` website at any time. In doing so, not only will they see current transactions, but blockchain.info will also display a list of all previous transactions associated with your bitcoin address. As a result, if someone knows your public wallet address, there is no real anonymity when it comes to using bitcoin, as all of your financial transactions are publicly visible.

This story changes a bit whenever bitcoin *exchanges* are involved (Chapter 2 talks more about exchanges). Anyone can see a transfer from your bitcoin wallet to the wallet address of the exchange, as these are publicly listed in most cases. However, if you sell your bitcoin, it becomes a lot harder to track where those coins went to. In that regard, there is a small sense of anonymity, but once again, it depends on your personal opinion as to how secure this is.

Introducing third-party anonymity

Ways to stay anonymous when using bitcoin do exist, though none of these methods is very user-friendly at this time. Generally speaking, those who are interested in anonymity may have something to hide. It could be that they are seeking to avoid paying taxes or that they are purchasing illegal goods or services in their jurisdiction. Using services such as an online wallet, you can "mix up" coins and extract them from a completely different address, without the addresses being linked together in any way. This technology is developing even as we type. But using such services involves a few risks, and if your coins are lost in the process, there is no way to get them back. Don't worry too much about losing your coins though — we explain more on how to manage them and your wallet in Chapter 5.

Always do your own research before using any external service and ask yourself whether or not anonymizing your BTC balance is really that important to you or not.

One of the biggest issues concerning external services is the fact you are relying on a third-party to anonymize your coins. Bitcoin and digital currency were created to remove any middleman from the equation and put the users in control of their funds at all times. Trusting a third party with your money essentially goes against bitcoin's core values. Plus, using an anonymity service for bitcoin raises suspicion of money laundering. Considering that you are already semi-anonymous by only exposing your public bitcoin address, taking things one step further could raise suspicions around your possible intentions. Chapter 5 covers more on how to manage your funds and the most appropriate ways to do this.

Protecting privacy

When it comes to protecting your privacy, the story is similar.

There are ways to protect your privacy when using bitcoin to move funds around, but these require some effort and planning:

✔ You can generate a new address for every individual transaction.

✔ You can avoid posting your public bitcoin wallet address in a public place.

Generating a new wallet

When receiving funds from another user, you can opt to give them a brand new, freshly generated wallet address, which cannot be directly linked to any existing addresses you already own. This type of *throwaway address* lets users isolate transactions from one another, which is the primary precaution you can take to protect your privacy.

However, depending on how you store your funds — which type of bitcoin client you are using and which operating system you're using it on — you may also be able to generate *change addresses*. For example, if you install the Bitcoin Core client on your computer or laptop, you can create a new change address every time you send funds to someone else.

A change address occurs whenever you have a certain amount of bitcoin in your wallet balance and are sending less than that total amount to another user. Let's say you have 3 bitcoin and need to spend 0.25 bitcoin. You need to receive the "change" — 2.75 bitcoin in this case — in your wallet. The Bitcoin Core client (as well as a few other desktop clients) allows you to have this "change" sent to a newly generated address. In doing so, there is no direct link between your original address and the new address, even though you can trace back the steps by looking at the blockchain itself.

Keeping your wallet address secret

Another way to protect your privacy — to a certain extent — is by not posting your public bitcoin wallet address in a public place. Using the address on your website, blog, social media, or on a forum is not a good idea if you want privacy. Once someone stumbles across your wallet address and can somehow tie it to you personally, there is no way to restore privacy other than by using one of the aforementioned methods.

Demonstrating fungibility

The main problem with bitcoin is its fungibility, or more correctly, lack thereof. *Fungibility* has nothing to do with mushrooms, by the way. It's just a fancy term for goods being interchangeable or capable of being substituted . . . and that suits bitcoin.

Most governments in the world will stick to their own, controllable system of issuing fiat currency. Local currencies are centralized and issued by a central bank. If they need more money, the central bank can simply issue more money by turning on the printing presses or engaging in quantitative easing as it's been termed. Thus, either by order of the government or by acting as an independent authority — a central bank may boost liquidity in the economy by carrying out quantitative easing. With bitcoin, this is not the case, as there is a fixed liquidity cap of 21 million coins. Thus, the cap of 21 million coins essentially means that bitcoin is not fungible as other fiat currencies are.

Trusting the Idea of Bitcoin

One of the biggest hurdles to overcome whenever a new technology comes knocking on your door is whether or not you should put your trust in it. In the case of bitcoin, that trust has to work on both sides. Even though you as the user are always in control of your own finances, you still have to trust the rest of the bitcoin network to not drop off the face of the earth tomorrow.

The chances of bitcoin disappearing are so slim that it isn't something you should worry about. However, if there is one thing that life has taught most of us, it is that there are no certainties in life. Luckily for everyone involved, the bitcoin network consists of many individual users, as well as *bitcoin nodes*, which are put in place to keep the network running at all times. We explain more about nodes and their role in Chapter 6.

This brings us to the concept about bitcoin that people have the most difficulty with in terms of trust: decentralization. As mentioned, bitcoin is a *decentralized digital currency,* which means there is no central point of failure that would cause the bitcoin network to not recover. Every individual user is an integral part of the bitcoin ecosystem, so it would take a nearly impossible amount of collaboration in order to shut down everyone at the same time.

You can compare bitcoin's decentralization with how Google's search engine works. The engine itself gets accessed by millions of people at the same time, yet it never seems to slow down. That's because Google's search engine runs on so many servers — in a decentralized manner — that it would take a tremendous effort to bring it down altogether.

Decentralization also brings forth another aspect that makes people think twice before getting involved in bitcoin. Because the network is made up of lots of individual users, there is no central authority overseeing the bitcoin network. That means if you own bitcoin and something goes wrong for some unforeseen reason, no one will reimburse you. Once your BTC are gone — either by you having spent them or even having lost them, they are gone — there is no chance to recover them.

Trusting bitcoin technology

Human nature tells us to keep doing things the way we have been doing them. Beware change. When the Internet came around in the early 1990s, few thought it would ever become a commonplace, household service. It was for geeks. Yet look where we are now — everybody's grandparents and their pet dogs are on the Internet. And we couldn't do without it. That being said, the transition from no connections to people all over the world being connected was a big change.

Bitcoin is often compared to the early Internet, a new and disruptive technology that seems to be far ahead of its time. In part, that's true, as bitcoin is solving a technological problem that most people don't think about in the first place. Not because the evidence isn't there, but simply because human nature rejects changes as long as things "still work fine the way they are."

And just like the Internet, it will take a rather long period, many years at least, before bitcoin becomes mainstream technology. Even though several great bitcoin projects and platforms are in development, it will take a lot of time until they are ready to be used by the general public. On top of that, there need to be more educational efforts regarding bitcoin that focus on the underlying ideas and technology, rather than the "alternative currency" aspect.

On the other hand, a lot of people have already put their trust in bitcoin technology. Most of the technology in existence today is focused on financial means, such as the remittance market. Bitcoin technology allows you to send money to anyone in the world, at little to no expense. In doing so, remittance players such as Western Union, Moneygram, and even traditional banks will potentially face stiff competition from this "fake Internet money," as bitcoin is often called.

 Whether you should put your trust in bitcoin technology is something only you can decide for yourself. Bitcoin was, is, and will always be intended to put you in control of your bitcoin money. If you decide to embrace that freedom, you have plenty of reading ahead of you in this book. We believe it will be worth your while.

Trusting bitcoin as currency

As previously noted, bitcoin is not a proper currency in its truest sense, but rather an alternative, digital method of payment. Granted, you can buy and sell services and goods in exchange for bitcoin, but the monetary aspect lacks certain features required for it to be considered as a true "currency" in the traditional meaning.

Nevertheless, lots of merchants put their trust in bitcoin as a payment method, simply by accepting it alongside more traditional ways of paying. The reasons are fairly simple:

✔ No extra costs associated with accepting bitcoin payments

✔ No additional infrastructure to set up

On top of that, as a merchant, you can integrate bitcoin payments in both your online and physical stores, if you want. In either case, you will be able to convert any bitcoin transaction to your preferred local currency immediately and have funds deposited to your bank account the next business day.

From a consumer point of view, using bitcoin as a payment method means you don't have to spend any of your cash, nor use a bank card or credit card linked to any of your bank accounts. However, in order to obtain bitcoin, you usually have to buy some first, which does involve spending your own money. Have no fear though — many other ways to earn bitcoin without investing your money up front are explored in Chapter 4.

Bitcoin is all about letting the individual user control funds at any given time. And that aspect scares a lot of people away, as governments and banks have been holding our hands along the way for the past half century or so. Taking care of everything ourselves can be a burden, as many do not want that responsibility. And if you honestly feel that you don't want to invest your time in managing your money at your leisure, when you need it, at any given time or place, then bitcoin is not for you.

But if you're fed up with the current financial system of governments and banks, bitcoin is well worth the time and effort. No one is saying that bitcoin has to replace the local currency you've been using to date. Both systems can coexist peacefully. However, once you start seeing the benefits and potential of using bitcoin for various types of purchases, you will feel a rush of excitement, and more importantly, invigorating financial freedom.

Chapter 2

Buying and Storing Bitcoins

● ●

In This Chapter

▶ Learning how to buy bitcoins

▶ Finding an exchange

▶ Getting verified

▶ Keeping your bitcoins safe

● ●

*T*his chapter looks at the practicalities of beginning to use bitcoin: getting your (virtual) hands on that all-important first bitcoin, setting up a way to store and spend it, and of course, being security conscious as you head off on your spending spree.

By the end of this chapter, you should be able to set up and get going with bitcoin.

Before getting started, you will need one or both of the following:

✔ Bitcoin Wallet software installed on your computer or laptop (downloaded from `https://bitcoin.org/en/choose-your-wallet`).

✔ Bitcoin Wallet software installed on your mobile device (downloaded from `https://bitcoin.org/en/choose-your-wallet`).

Getting Started: How to Obtain Bitcoins

The first hurdle to overcome when getting involved in bitcoin is how to obtain bitcoins. Although you can do so using several methods — which we'll look at in this chapter — the most obvious choice is to buy them.

But where do you go when trying to buy a digital token in exchange for physical money? These platforms are called *exchanges*, and just like an exchange office where you can use local currency to obtain foreign currency, bitcoin exchanges exchange your physical money for bitcoins.

A *bitcoin exchange* is the currency's equivalent of the services offered by banks or other regulated institutions that allow currency exchange — commonly known as FOREX transactions. You may have an account at the bitcoin exchange where you hold funds in your local currency and you use that account to trade for bitcoins. From that account, you would send the bitcoins to your preferred wallet and use the bitcoins as you see fit — similar to how you would use local fiat currency held in your checking account.

If you recall, bitcoin was designed to work as a borderless, decentralized payment method without needing to convert to local currencies in order to be used. And although a lot of goods and services may be purchased with bitcoin, the need to convert bitcoins (also called BTC) to local currency to pay bills and whatnot is still there. This is why we need exchanges — to help facilitate these types of transfers.

Getting registered on an exchange

A bitcoin exchange usually takes the form of a website, though there are a few physical exchanges out there (discussed later on in this chapter). When it comes to choosing an exchange, you've got plenty of choice of providers. Depending on your geographical location and the type of fiat currency you use, certain exchanges may be preferable to others. At this time, there is no bitcoin exchange that services all countries in the world, due to legal reasons. We recommend checking out the list of exchanges linked from the Bitcoin.org website or reviewing a current guide from an online news site such as Coindesk.

You can check them out here:

```
https://howtobuybitcoins.info/#!/
```

```
www.coindesk.com/information/how-can-i-buy-
bitcoins/
```

The main goal of any bitcoin exchange platform is to facilitate the transfer from and to physical currency to and from digital currencies, such as bitcoin.

Anyone can create an account at a bitcoin exchange without having to buy bitcoins at that time or owning bitcoins beforehand.

Here's the way an online bitcoin exchange works (the actual details will vary depending on the exchange you sign up to):

1. You sign up for a user account by providing basic information.

2. You then receive an e-mail in your mailbox to activate your account.

3. Once you have activated your account, the actual registration process begins.

 As you might expect from exchange services, they are the leading indicators of how current market prices are fluctuating. In the case of bitcoin exchanges, these prices can fluctuate by quite a bit, as each business runs on a slightly different business model. Some bitcoin exchanges will pay you less when selling bitcoin and ask a slightly lower market price when you want to buy bitcoin. Other exchange platforms will offer you the current market value but take a small cut (0.05–0.5 percent) per executed transaction as commission.

Even though bitcoin is all about supply and demand based on the open market, buyers and sellers still need to be connected. Most bitcoin exchanges use a *trading engine,* which automatically matches buy and sell orders on both sides of the order book. However, there are other options too, such as local peer-to-peer trades, covered later in this chapter.

A very important aspect of bitcoin exchanges is the fact that some — though not all — platforms allow you to exchange BTC to a global currency that is not necessarily your local currency. For example, if you live in China, your local currency is the Chinese Yuan. However, if you want to get your hands on U.S. dollars (USD), euros (EUR), or British pounds (GBP), you may choose to use a bitcoin exchange trading in those currency pairs.

 When attempting to make a withdrawal to your bank account, the value may still be converted to your local currency if your bank doesn't accept foreign currency transfers. Always do some research before attempting these types of transfers and make sure you are prepared for any associated risks in doing so.

Bitcoin exchanges are obliged by their local laws and respective national regulators of financial services and products to obtain some of your personal information. This information includes, but is not limited to, your full name, address, phone number (mobile and/or landline) and country of residence. On top of that, most bitcoin exchanges require you to fill in your date of birth, which is part of the identity verification process (see the next section).

Know-Your-Customer: Passing the KYC

In order to properly use a bitcoin exchange, you will need to complete a "Know-Your-Customer" (KYC) verification procedure. This process sounds a lot scarier than it really is, even though you are obligated to submit some very delicate information related to you as a person.

Step 1: Confirming your phone number

The first step is verifying your mobile phone number. Most bitcoin exchanges send you a text message to that phone number with a code. That code needs to be entered on a specific page during the verification process in order to verify that you have access to that mobile number in case of an emergency, or during an account's password-recovery process.

Step 2: Providing personal ID

The next step usually requires you to verify your identity by providing a copy of personal identification. Depending on the bitcoin exchange platform you're using, these documents can range from a scan of your ID or driver's license and a recent utility bill, to a copy of your birth certificate or passport.

The types of ID documents required depend on how much you are expecting to trade through your bitcoin exchange. Larger amounts require stricter verification, and thus more sensitive personal information.

And this is one of the major struggles novice users face when verifying their identity and purchasing bitcoins for the first time. Besides the information that needs to be submitted, there's also a waiting period that must be taken into account before these documents are verified. Most major bitcoin exchanges get these documents reviewed within a few hours, but there have been reports of delays taking up to a week.

 Whenever you submit any documents, always make sure everything is clearly legible, as this will make the verification process a lot smoother.

Figuring out exchange rates

Bitcoin exchange rates to and from a country's physical currency may vary quite a lot. Not only do rates depend on the time of day during which you're looking to make a trade, but there's a massive difference between various exchange platforms.

The bitcoin exchange business is very competitive in nature, and every platform is looking to attract as many customers as possible. In order to do so, each bitcoin exchange has to come up with its own business model to cater to as many people as possible. In most cases, the novice users are the largest untapped market, and efforts are focused on making bitcoin more accessible.

To get the best exchange rates for yourself, follow these tips:

✔ Whenever you're looking to exchange bitcoin for physical currency or vice versa, make sure to check the current bitcoin price first. See the nearby sidebar "Keeping an eye on exchange rates" for further details. Over the past few years, bitcoin exchanges have started offering a "fixed" price per bitcoin, assuming you complete the transaction within a certain time frame. For example, when converting BTC into local currency, a user must complete the transfer within the next 15 minutes in order to get the current price. Failure to do so may result in a different price at the time of transaction, which can be either higher or lower.

✔ Keep a close eye on the bitcoin exchange rate for your local currency at all times, to maximize your profits and reduce your losses. Although Bitcoinwisdom.com is undoubtedly one of our favorite sources of data, there are other similar sources such as Cryptrader.com and Coinmarketcap.com. Whichever tools you choose to use, they can aid you by giving you charts such as you would expect to see in regular fiat currency conversions, or just a flat BTC/local currency rate in digits. See the nearby sidebar on exchange rates for more info. You can check them out here:

`https://bitcoinwisdom.com`

`https://cryptrader.com`

`http://coinmarketcap.com/currencies/`

✔ Keep in mind that there will usually be an exchange fee at some point during the transaction, so be sure to understand how much that will be. Some bitcoin exchange platforms take a small cut when your buy or sell order has been executed, whereas others will simply charge you more or pay you less overall. Plus, additional fees may be applicable when withdrawing your physical currency to a bank account or other payment method.

Keeping an eye on exchange rates

Depending on which platform you are using, there are various methods at your disposal to keep an eye on the current bitcoin exchange rate. For computer users, the best option is to check the Bitcoin Wisdom website at `www.bitcoinwisdom.com`. On this platform, you will find real time bitcoin price statistics for all major currencies (USD, EUR, CAD, RUR, and CNY), and the most popular exchanges dealing with those specific currencies.

For mobile users, the story is quite different. Most mobile bitcoin wallets show the fiat currency value next to your bitcoin value inside the app itself (see Chapter 5 for more details on mobile wallets). This is a great way to give you an idea of how much your coins are worth at any given time. Keep in mind you will need an active Internet connection — either mobile data or wi-fi — for this price to reflect the current value.

Exchange rates on bitcoin exchanges fluctuate constantly, in part attributable to free market supply and demand. In recent years, the overall trading volume of bitcoin has increased exponentially, with most of the trading taking place in China and the United States. Despite all of that, other local exchange rates around the world may go up when the major bitcoin markets are going down, or the other way around.

Understanding peer-to-peer versus regular exchanges

Two types of bitcoin exchanges are in use: *peer-to-peer* and what we'll call *regular*.

On the one hand, there are the regular bitcoin exchanges, which use an order book to match buy and sell orders between people. However, neither the buyer nor the seller has any idea who the other party is, and this provides all users with a certain level of anonymity and privacy protection. This is the most commonly used form of exchanging local currency to and from its digital counterpart in the form of bitcoin.

However, bitcoin was originally created to enable peer-to-peer transactions. Unlike other familiar peer-to-peer technologies you may be familiar with, such as torrent applications, in the bitcoin domain peer-to-peer means a one-on-one relationship. A *peer-to-peer transaction* means that you have data related to the person or entity you're interacting with at all times, rather than interacting with several different peers, as in the case of torrents. The information you have on that person can range from a bitcoin wallet address, to their forum username, location, IP address, or can even involve a face-to-face meeting.

Rather than using an order book to match up buy and sell orders — and thus controlling all the funds being used on the exchange platform itself — peer-to-peer exchanges match buyers and sellers without holding any funds during the trade.

For example, let's say you want to buy a bitcoin from someone who lives in the same city as you do. Rather than hoping to stumble across that person on a traditional exchange — chances of that are slim to none — you can initiate a peer-to-peer transfer with that individual. There are several bitcoin platforms in existence that allow you to register an account in order to find other bitcoin enthusiasts in your local area. Some of the more popular platforms include Gemini.com for the U.S. market, whereas Bitstamp.net and Kraken.com offer facilities for customers in international markets subject to their individual policies and restrictions. You can check them out here:

```
https://gemini.com

www.bitstamp.net

https://kraken.com
```

That said, not everyone will be willing to meet up face-to-face. Some people prefer a payment by traditional means, such as a bank transfer or PayPal, rather than meet up for a cash transaction.

Depending on what kind of trading experience you prefer, peer-to-peer trading may be more suitable for your needs than the regular exchange. Generally, peer-to-peer trades do not require you to provide any documentation regarding your identity and offer a reputation system in order to track your own — and other users' — trading history. In doing so, your chances of completing a trade successfully will only increase.

One of the most interesting aspects about peer-to-peer bitcoin exchanges is their built-in reputation system. Because you're dealing with other traders directly, whose funds are not overseen by the platform owners themselves, the trust element is more important than ever before. It only makes sense to know a little bit more about traders' previous history before going into business with them.

Storing Your Bitcoins: Being Safe While Using Exchanges

One of the first things you should keep in mind when you consider storing your bitcoins on an exchange platform is that it involves quite a lot of security risks.

It goes against the very ideology of bitcoin to use middlemen and be dependent on centralized services and platforms. And even though these exchanges deal in decentralized digital currency, the platforms themselves, like banks, still represent central points of failure, which makes them incredibly vulnerable to attack. That said, bitcoin developers are not sitting on their hands — see the sidebar "Guarding Fort Bitcoin" for info on what they're doing to protect your funds.

Unfortunately for bitcoin users around the world, exchanges do not have the best of reputations when it comes to storing your digital wealth. Whenever an exchange is hacked, or the owners decide to run off with the money, there is not much that can be done, except trying to file legal action and hope the matter is investigated sooner rather than later. When you put your money in a bank, you are protected by government insurance — for example, in the U.S., the Federal Deposit Insurance Corporation (FDIC) insures your deposits up to $100,000. Not the case when it comes to bitcoin exchanges.

By storing your bitcoin on an exchange platform, you are not only trusting the service to stay online at all times — which usually will be the case, but you never know — you also rely on the platform being secure enough. To put that into perspective: You are putting your faith — and your financial wealth — in the hands of a platform that claims to use sufficient security measures in order to protect your data and money.

Luckily for the bitcoin world, exchanges have stepped up their security game in recent years, even though there is never such a thing as a bullet-proof platform. As is always the case with new and disruptive technology, it takes time to fully understand its potential and how it should be properly protected. And in the past, exchange platforms had to learn that the hard — and costly — way.

Even though bitcoin exchanges have become far more secure than they were in 2010, that doesn't mean they should be treated as an online wallet service (see Chapter 5 for more on wallets). Bitcoin users have plenty of options at their disposal to store BTC in a decentralized and more secure manner. That said, centralized wallets such as those provided by Blockchain.info or Coinbase.com are popular as mobile solutions.

Guarding Fort Bitcoin

In the original bitcoin whitepaper (`https://bitcoin.org/bitcoin.pdf`), as presented by Satoshi Nakamoto, are details on how bitcoin technology can offer tremendous security improvements compared to the current banking infrastructure. It would take quite some time until we saw the first developments in that area. For example, a tool like multi-signature security was only implemented in 2013.

Multi-signature security in the world of bitcoin is similar to security for traditional banking. Rather than entrusting one single person or entity with access to a certain wallet, multiple "keys" are distributed to various parties.

For example: Mark and Alice want to open up a joint bitcoin wallet. In order to ensure there is an unbiased "arbitrator," they decide to give Dave a key as well. During the wallet-creation process, a total of three private keys are generated. One key belongs to Mark, another to Alice, and a third key to Dave for safekeeping. If either Mark or Alice wants to send a bitcoin transaction, they need to convince each other or one of them needs to convince Dave that this is a good idea.

In practical terms, a multi-signature bitcoin wallet means that multiple parties must agree and sign off on the transaction with their key. In this case, either Mark and Alice, or Alice and Dave, or Mark and Dave need to come to an agreement before any funds can be spent from the bitcoin wallet. If only one party wants to and the two other disagree, the transaction can't be executed.

More information can be found at `https://en.bitcoin.it/wiki/Multisignature`.

That said, protecting a financial platform — which is what bitcoin exchanges are — is not an easy feat. Quite a lot of costs are involved in terms of hiring security experts, testing new features, shutting down trading when a discrepancy occurs, and so on. All in all, security and monitoring are a 24/7 job.

One of the additions to bitcoin exchange security comes in the form of two-factor authentication. Though this security feature is completely optional, it is advisable for all users to enable two-factor authentication (2FA) on their bitcoin exchange account. (We talk more about 2FA later in this chapter.)

Bitcoin exchanges have started to implement multi-signature bitcoin wallets themselves as well. If a hacker were to breach a bitcoin exchange, transferring the funds out is nearly impossible, as they would need other keyholders to sign off on every transaction. However, not all of a bitcoin exchange's funds are stored in cold storage multi-signature wallets. (More on this topic later in this chapter).

Long story short, storing bitcoin on an exchange platform for long periods of time isn't very secure. However, if you are planning to spend or transfer those coins within the next 48 hours, it is relatively safe to store them in the exchange wallet for the time being. Any period longer than that, and you're putting yourself at a major risk.

The best way to store your bitcoins is on a wallet in your control, regardless of whether it is on a computer or a mobile device. See Chapter 5 for more.

Bitcoin is designed to give end-users full control of their funds, and no one should rely on a third-party service to keep their coins safe. Transfer your funds from a bitcoin exchange or online wallet to the bitcoin wallet software on your computer or mobile device as soon as possible.

Using two-factor authentication (2FA)

Even if you aren't planning to store bitcoins on an exchange for an extended period of time, you may want to look into ways to protect your account. Most (non-bitcoin) online services require users to authenticate with just a username and password, which is not exactly the most secure way of protecting your credentials and personal information.

In recent years, it has become apparent that more layers of security need to be implemented on top of the standard authentication protocols. One of the more popular solutions to tackle this problem is called *two-factor authentication* (2FA), which requires an additional "token" to be entered when accessing your account. Failing to enter the correct combination results in an error message.

It's not uncommon for an unauthorized third party to get access to your username and password credentials. This is not always a fault of the individual, as some online services may use unsecure methods of storing these details. Enabling 2FA adds a layer of security on top of that to safeguard your data and money.

2FA may be used in multiple ways, although not all of these forms are supported by every platform. The most common type of 2FA comes in the form of Google Authenticator, which is an application you can install on any mobile device. Using Google Authenticator is quite simple. After you download the app to your mobile device, you set up a new account:

1. Log in to the service or platform you want to protect with 2FA.

2. Scan an associated QR code with the camera of your mobile device.

3. Use that QR code to link to your authentication details, pairing it to your mobile device.

Every time you open Google Authenticator, it generates a new 2FA code for your account. These codes remain valid for a very short period of time, after which a new code is automatically generated. The validation of this code is automatically verified when logging in. Entering an expired code will return you back to the login screen.

Even though mobile 2FA sounds very convenient, a couple of drawbacks should be kept in mind:

✔ You need to carry your mobile device with you at all times, and it needs to be charged with enough battery to generate a 2FA code. This will not be an issue for most people, but it can cause inconvenience at certain times.

✔ If you lose your phone or it gets stolen, you also lose your 2FA credentials. Even though there ways to remove 2FA security from your account and enable it on a new device, doing so is quite the hassle and not a process you want to run through if it's not necessary.

Other ways to authenticate your account through 2FA include services like Clef and Authy, available from the relevant app store for your mobile device, and even plain old SMS verification. However, these options — except for SMS verification — require you to carry additional hardware on you in order to verify your credentials, making them less convenient.

SMS verification also has its own drawbacks. For example, if you are in an area where you get bad to no cellular signals, SMS verification for 2FA purposes won't work. Plus, if you are in a foreign country, additional fees may be charged to you for receiving the 2FA authentication code.

Regardless of which option you decide to use, when it comes to bitcoin exchanges, be sure to enable any form of 2FA you possibly can. This protects your account properly, and even though it may be slightly cumbersome at times, protecting your money is well worth going the extra mile.

Understanding liability

The topic of liability regarding bitcoin exchanges is a gray area at best. We'll do our best to explain your liability here.

Bitcoin is an unregulated and ungoverned digital currency, which makes any associated services fall under the same category by default. However, depending on which part of the world you offer that bitcoin exchange service to, there are some regulations you will have to adhere to.

At the time of writing, it remains unclear as to who is liable when your bitcoin exchange is hacked or when the service shuts down all of a sudden. Most of the bigger, more reputable exchanges have systems in place that protect you from financial risk up to a certain amount. The idea is that, if the exchange gets breached, or your funds are lost in any other way while stored on the platform, the exchange will reimburse you out of its pocket. That said, we advise you to take a sensible approach and only store on exchanges what you need and not treat them as secure storage for your bitcoins.

Some economists would go as far as saying that a bitcoin exchange is a self-regulating platform, such as NASDAQ. However, as big as the NASDAQ is, it claims immunity from computer crashes — meaning it will not reimburse any funds lost due to a computer crash. Bitcoin exchanges operate in a different manner, but with no clear regulator to report to, there is never a guarantee you will get your money back.

The amount of protection that exchanges may offer to customers may well depend on where they are registered and the licensing requirements (or lack thereof) for the exchanges to operate in that jurisdiction. Storing your bitcoins on an exchange for more than a day or two is never a good idea, and if that exchange were to cease operating for any reason at all, your options will be determined by the local laws of the jurisdiction where the exchange is registered. Generally speaking, the tougher the licensing requirements for an exchange, the more protection you're likely to be offered. However, you should verify the details of any exchange that you choose to use and the level of protection that it may or may not offer you. Granted, you may be able to take legal action should the worst come to pass, but a lawsuit is very costly and time-consuming.

More and more bitcoin exchanges have opened the door to receive independent third-party audits. An auditor can verify whether a bitcoin exchange is solvent enough to continue its operations, and if needed, get the security measures stress-tested to verify whether or not user data is protected properly. We discuss current legislative efforts in more details in Chapter 9.

Every exchange has its own way of publishing audit results. To find more information regarding the audit report of your preferred bitcoin exchange, contact its support via live chat or e-mail. A representative will be able to give you a clear answer on whether or not the company conducts audits and where the results are published.

Regardless of how you look at it, in the end, all liability lies with the people using bitcoin exchanges. Bitcoin puts financial control back in your hands, and if you decide to store bitcoins on an exchange platform, they are your sole responsibility in the end.

Encrypting Your Bitcoins

Security is a very important aspect of the bitcoin world — without the proper security in place, your digital wealth could get stolen at any time. Bitcoin Core developers have taken notice of this problem from the beginning and enabled a feature inside the bitcoin client that lets you "encrypt" your wallet by protecting it with a passphrase (see Chapter 5 for more on bitcoin wallets).

Bitcoin Core is the "standard" bitcoin software client for computer users. All other bitcoin software wallets are based on Bitcoin Core and provide a different user interface and/or bring additional features to the table.

Choosing a passphrase

By using a passphrase, you "lock" your coins from being spent. Even if an attacker were to gain access to the device on which your bitcoin wallet is running, they would not be able to do anything with the funds unless they also had your passphrase.

Your sensitive bitcoin information — a file called wallet.dat that holds the digital ownership of your BTC — is not encrypted by default. This means that if you just install the bitcoin client on a computer or laptop, it isn't protected. As soon as someone gains access to your computer, they can spend your coins instantly.

Therefore, you should properly encrypt your bitcoin wallet. The latest Bitcoin Core client contains a feature that encrypts your wallet with a passphrase. Or if you prefer, you can use an external tool to encrypt your wallet.dat file, most of which are completely free of charge to use. Keep in mind that you need to enter the passphrase every time you want to access your funds or look at a transaction. Encrypting a bitcoin wallet restricts it to "spectator" mode, in which you can see the balance and incoming transactions, but nothing else in detail.

All bitcoin users should encrypt their bitcoin client, and the best code of conduct is to use a very strong and difficult-to-crack password — preferably a password that contains numbers, upper- and lowercase letters, and even symbols such as @ or #. This password should seem as random as possible to anyone else, but keep in mind you have to enter it manually every time you want to use your bitcoin wallet to its full potential.

If you want to encrypt a mobile bitcoin wallet, the process is slightly different. Most mobile applications store the wallet.dat file — or its mobile counterpart — on the device itself and protect it with a PIN code. Though PIN codes are generally less secure than encryptions keys, they provide enough security for most users. However, you can always look into encrypting mobile wallets as well. Find software solutions using keywords typed into your favorite search engine, such as 7Zip, Axcrypt, TrueCrypt, or lrzip.

Beware malware

Something every bitcoin user needs to keep in mind at all times is that, regardless of whether you encrypt your wallet or not, there is no such thing as a completely safe and secure environment.

Most bitcoin users will already have antivirus software installed on their computer, but once you start saving financial data on your machine — including bitcoin — you should add more layers of security to your system.

Computer users need to protect themselves against all kinds of harmful programs and software. Just installing an antivirus program on its own is no longer sufficient, especially when bitcoin wallets are being used. You'll also need an anti-malware and anti-spyware program, of which there are many available on the Internet, such as Bitdefender, Kaspersky, and Norton Antivirus products. Note that although these examples cited are termed *antivirus* products, they contain a wide range of features to protect you from the many security threats on the Internet.

A major threat plaguing bitcoin wallets around the world is malware. *Malware* is a particularly nasty kind of software infection, because the end-user usually doesn't even notice its presence until it is too late. There are different forms of malware, each of which can lead to you losing your bitcoins if you're not protecting yourself with the proper software tools. Malware can be spread through your online behavior when you visit sites with malicious content (usually adult-related), click the wrong links on the Internet, open suspicious e-mail attachments, or download illegal material. Each of these events may pose a serious threat to your computer and your bitcoin wallet, and should be avoided at all costs.

Not every e-mail you receive contains malicious files or images, and you shouldn't start to become paranoid about every e-mail you open. But if you have no idea who the sender is, don't open any attachment in that e-mail. Clicking a suspicious link is harder to spot, as it can even appear on your social media pages (especially Facebook and Twitter, which are quite prone to these types of links, and disaster is just one mouse click away).

Spyware is often compared to computer viruses, even though there are notable differences between the two. Spyware logs information, such as which websites and corresponding login details have been used, which software you have installed on your computer, and what kinds of e-mails you've sent and received. This is extremely worrying for people using online bitcoin services, as spyware can obtain your login details and someone can take advantage of that information.

A proper anti-malware and anti-spyware software solution is usually not free, even though most can be tested without charge for a period of time. But if you're really taking the plunge to take back financial control and manage your money yourself using bitcoin, security is your number one priority.

Storing physical bitcoin

Rather than storing your bitcoins on a computer or mobile device, a third option is fairly common among digital currency users. *Physical bitcoins* — yes, they do exist — are not just great collector's items, they also let you store your digital currency on them. Or to be more precise, most of them do.

Different types of physical bitcoins exist, just as currencies have coins of different monetary values. The nearby sidebar "The Casascius Series of physical bitcoins" highlights one particular, popular line.

Each physical coin has its own price, and they come in various alloys. The most common physical bitcoins these days are minted in silver, although there is quite a selection of both bronze and golden coins on the market as well. All coins require a small upfront investment and can be seen as both a collector's item and bitcoin vault at the same time.

The Casascius series of physical bitcoins

Perhaps the most famous "line" of physical bitcoins is the Casascius series, created by Mike Caldwell. Over the years, there have been several generations of these coins, all of which can be funded by the buyer using bitcoin. For example, a physical 0.5 BTC coin can be funded by 0.5 bitcoin. You should aim to fund these coins for no more than their face value.

The main reason Casascius coins are so popular is because every edition had a limited mintage, and all the non-commemorative coins are made of silver or gold. Additionally, several Casascius coins have had "errors" on them, which make them even more valuable from a collector's point of view.

More information on Casascius coins can be found at `https://en.bitcoin.it/wiki/Casascius_physical_bitcoins`.

Most physical bitcoins allow the user to store a bitcoin wallet address, and its private key is in the back of the coin. In doing so, you are officially "funding" the coin by sending a BTC amount to that designated address. All coins come with funding instructions, so for the most up-to-date information on funding, read that small print!

Keep in mind that you are responsible for generating this address and the associated private key yourself, so make sure you are the only one who has access to those details.

Once you have created your bitcoin wallet address and private key, you'll also receive a small piece of paper on which this confirmation is printed. This document usually comes with the coin itself and includes a hologram. That hologram has to be placed over the back of the coin, making sure your wallet information isn't tampered with (tampering would break the hologram).

Many people use physical coins to store some spare bitcoin in the hopes of an increase in BTC price in the future. Plus, these coins cannot be spent unless they break the hologram and retrieve the private key.

Funding a physical bitcoin is a great way to keep your spending habits under control.

Buying Bitcoins in Person

Buying bitcoins in person is a great way to venture into the world of digital currency. Buying in person not only gets you acquainted with peer-to-peer transfer, but is also a way to meet some new and like-minded people with an interest in bitcoin.

In-person bitcoin trades *can* attract unwanted attention from people when there is cash involved. Thieves have become more aware of bitcoin trades being completed in person, and someone walking about with a lot of cash is a perfect target for such individuals.

Before you can complete your peer-to-peer trade, you need to prepare some important things. Perhaps the most important aspect of completing any form of bitcoin trading is creating your wallet address. After all, without a valid bitcoin wallet address, there is no way to store your BTC.

Your bitcoin wallet address

Your bitcoin wallet is actually a long string of random numbers and lower- and uppercase letters. It is impossible to remember a wallet address by heart, and that is intended. The reason for this is simple: additional security. If someone were to remember your bitcoin address, they could look it up on the blockchain and monitor your bitcoin activity in real-time, for instance on www.blockchain.info.

You may create a bitcoin wallet address in several ways, but if you're completing a peer-to-peer trade, mobile solutions might be your best bet. By installing any of the many mobile bitcoin wallet apps, the address generation process is usually taken care of for you. But keep in mind that you may need to register before using a certain app, so make sure to complete that part beforehand.

A bitcoin wallet address will be automatically generated for you once you install the bitcoin software on your computer or mobile device.

Once you are set up and ready to go out, there's one last thing to complete. During your peer-to-peer bitcoin transaction, you need to present your bitcoin wallet address in a convenient manner to the person who is selling the coins to you. Rather than write down your bitcoin wallet address — a long string of random characters — here's a far better alternative: QR codes. You have probably seen these weird-looking square black-and-white codes on product packaging or on TV. Your bank may use them as well to authenticate mobile payments in a store nearby. QR codes are a great way of sharing bitcoin payment details with other users.

By creating a QR code, you can easily share your bitcoin wallet address with other users. All the other parties need to do is use their phone camera to scan the QR code into their installed bitcoin wallet app. All the details to complete the transaction on their end are filled automatically.

Not only is the use of QR codes for bitcoin transfers user-friendly, it's also less time-consuming and improves the overall user experience. After all, who wants to carry a laptop everywhere?

Another advantage of using QR codes is that the seller can show you that a transaction has been sent on their device, and by the time you check your device, the money has appeared. Keep in mind that every bitcoin transaction generally takes six network confirmations before the money becomes spendable.

Bitcoin transactions need to be confirmed on the network before the funds become spendable by the recipient. Every time a new block is found on the network — roughly every ten minutes — a transaction gains one additional confirmation. In some cases, it takes up to an hour before a bitcoin transaction becomes spendable.

Depending on which bitcoin wallet software you use, transactions may become spendable much faster. Especially on mobile devices, your funds are accessible a lot quicker than via computer. This is different for every type of bitcoin wallet, even though the "norm" is to have six network confirmations on a transaction before the funds can be moved again. Chapter 6 talks more about this.

Meeting in public places

Meeting up for a peer-to-peer bitcoin trade is best done in a public area. That protects both parties from potential harm — just in case. Plus, it's easy to navigate to a public place, even if you have never been there before.

 Pick a meeting place where you feel secure, preferably somewhere that's not directly linked to you personally. Don't invite anyone to your home or workplace, or any other place you frequently visit. Most bitcoin traders intend no harm, but you can never be sure.

 Another reason why public places are a better choice is that, in order to complete a bitcoin transfer, both users need access to an Internet connection. Plenty of places like coffee shops offer free wi-fi. In some cases, there may even be a network accessible throughout the entire city.

And of course, most mobile providers in the United States, Europe, and Asia offer data connectivity so long as you get a somewhat decent network signal. Once again, this makes public places good choices, compared to remote areas, where cellular connectivity may be an issue.

 Conducting a peer-to-peer bitcoin trade always comes with a small risk. People *have* been held at gunpoint in an attempt to steal their bitcoins. But this is extremely rare. Use common sense and exercise caution, especially if your bitcoin trader comes running up in a black-and-white stripy shirt carrying a bag marked SWAG.

Paying premium rates

Buying bitcoin in person from another user has the possibility of one major downside: You may end up paying a premium rate per bitcoin. This means that the price you pay to the person selling the bitcoin may be slightly higher compared to the actual exchange rate.

Not all bitcoin traders have a real idea as to what the current bitcoin value is across major exchanges. Checking the current value before agreeing to a peer-to-peer-trade is a good habit to get into. Not only does this give you better insight into how the bitcoin market works, it helps you get the most bitcoins for your money.

Bitcoin exchange rates work both ways, of course: No law prevents you from charging a premium rate as a bitcoin seller. This's the beautiful part about a free market based on supply and demand of bitcoins — anyone can set his own prices. Buyers will always be looking to buy as cheaply as possible, but if the seller's price happens to be the most convenient at that time, buyers will gladly pay a (small) premium.

How big this premium price may be depends on the seller entirely. Similar to how bitcoin ATMs operate (see nearby sidebar), a 5 percent premium on top of the current exchange rate is no exception. But you might encounter vastly different rates as well. It is a free market after all. Always be prepared to pay a price above the current exchange rate, as this is a small sacrifice you make in order to conveniently buy bitcoins compared to going through a lengthy verification process and sending a wire transfer.

Choosing a payment method

Completing a peer-to-peer bitcoin purchase means you have a somewhat wider selection of payment methods at your disposal. However, as people already agree to meet up in person, they will probably tell you which payment method they prefer. In most cases, the obvious choice will be fiat currency in hand.

Which brings us to what makes these in-person trades slightly dangerous. If you are planning to buy any amount of bitcoin worth less than a four-digit amount in your local currency, you should be relatively safe. Never conduct a person-to-person trade in the hopes of buying thousands of USD, EUR, or GBP worth of bitcoin and paying in cash — that would most likely get you in trouble.

Bitcoin ATMs

A bitcoin ATM works like a regular bank ATM with some differences. By using a bitcoin ATM, you can buy bitcoin in exchange for fiat currency. Some bitcoin ATMs also let you sell bitcoin in exchange for fiat currency. Every bitcoin ATM operates on a certain fee percentage, which can be anywhere from 0 to 12 percent.

More information on bitcoin ATM's can be found at `https://en.wikipedia.org/wiki/Bitcoin_ATM`.

Some local bitcoin sellers may accept a bank transfer and will pass along the details to you when bringing a laptop with you or visiting a bank ATM. However, this payment method is rarely used, for obvious reasons. If they wanted to accept a bank transfer, there would be no real need to meet up in person to begin with.

Using a payment method such as PayPal or a credit card will, in most cases, never be an option when completing an in-person bitcoin trade. The reason for that is simple: Both PayPal and credit cards can be used to charge back funds, whereas bitcoin transactions cannot. As a result, you could in theory buy bitcoin using PayPal or a credit card, receive the coins, and then ask for a refund through either the bank or PayPal. In most cases, you would actually get the money back as well.

Hot Wallets and Cold Storage

When talking about bitcoin exchange platforms, two terms you will encounter along the way are *cold storage* and *hot wallet*.

Both cold storage and the hot wallet are security measures put in place by exchange platforms to safeguard user funds from any mishap:

✓ **Cold storage refers to bitcoins kept offline.** You could compare this principle to banks moving customer funds into a vault rather than keeping it at the bank teller desk. In the case of bitcoin cold storage, though, there are other layers of security in place. Examples of cold storage include bitcoins kept on a USB drive or a dedicated hardware wallet.

As you may have guessed by now, most bitcoin wallets are stored on servers connected to the Internet. Cold storage wallets are kept entirely offline at all times, which also protects from harm in case a hacker would attempt to breach the platform.

Bitcoin exchange platforms protect the majority of — or, in some cases, all — customers from harm. However, there has to be sufficient bitcoin *liquidity* (amount of funds available at all times) within the exchange at all times as well, as there are always users who want to make a bitcoin withdrawal. And a proper exchange will process that withdrawal request immediately, rather than delaying it by several hours.

✓ *Hot wallet* **refers to the method by which every bitcoin exchange keeps a certain liquidity just in case there is a massive influx of withdrawal requests.** You may think of this liquidity as similar to the cash reserve that any bank must hold so that customers can access their funds at any point in time. This hot wallet provides liquidity of digital currency at all times. Unlike cold storage, a hot wallet is a bitcoin wallet connected to the Internet 24/7.

Good business practice for a bitcoin exchange means it never stores too many funds in a hot wallet. Even if it stores only 1 percent of the total amount of bitcoins circulating on the exchange, that can quickly add up to several hundreds or thousands of BTC. And if the platform were to be breached, the loss of funds would be quite catastrophic.

On top of that, most bitcoin exchange platforms will not process large bitcoin withdrawals from their hot wallet either, but rather move funds from cold storage to the intended recipient. Every platform has its own internal limits for doing so, making it hard to judge what is quantifiable as a *large amount* (but as mentioned earlier, you should never store too many BTC on an exchange wallet to begin with).

Securing user funds

Protecting user funds is priority number one for all bitcoin exchanges. If there were even one report of a user losing funds because of insufficient security measures, an exchange's reputation would be tarnished forever. And as always, bad news travels a lot faster than good news.

To protect customer funds, bitcoin exchanges are using other countermeasures besides cold storage and hot wallets (see the previous section), even though these are the two most common methods. There's still plenty of room for improvement, and several brilliant minds are collaborating to create a Bitcoin Exchange Security Standard.

This standard would improve the overall security of bitcoin exchanges and wallet providers and also set the table for minimum requirements every platform has to adhere to. In the past, not all bitcoin exchanges focused enough on security, which led to multiple hacks, breaches, and a lot of funds being stolen.

In its current form, there are ten standardized approaches to how private keys and master seeds are generated, as well as the handling of cold storage and hot wallets. A large focus is also put on security audits, proof-of-reserve, and other concepts that have not yet been unveiled.

Rather than have every exchange doing its own thing in terms of security and protecting customer funds, a unified standard gives bitcoin exchange a more legitimate status. This approach has led to some great success stories in recent years, which is part of the evolution of bitcoin's ecosystem.

Furthermore, a unified standard would be of great aid to regulators. Bitcoin is being kept under close watch by regulators all around the world, so it would be in the best interest of the bitcoin community to help them as much as we can. Regulators are tasked with developing frameworks for bitcoin's financial activities, and if there is a standard in place for exchange platforms, it could be of great benefit to all parties involved.

Preventing exchange hacks

Bitcoin exchanges have often been targeted by hackers intending to steal BTC. And over the course of the years, vast sums of money have fallen into the wrong hands, most of which can be attributed to a lack of security on these platforms.

Some of the most notorious exchange hacks in the world of bitcoin date all the way back to the very first time Mt. Gox (a Tokyo-based bitcoin exchange that has customers all over the world) became the victim of a hack. One of the website's accounts was compromised, ultimately leading to a global price crash from roughly U.S. $32 per bitcoin down to pennies. However, the hackers ran into Mt. Gox's daily withdrawal limit of $1,000 at that time, rendering their entire operation nearly useless.

Bitcoinica was a popular bitcoin exchange back in 2012, but that reputation took a major hit when the company lost thousands of bitcoins belonging to customers. Promises were made to pay back customers in full, from Bitcoinica's own pocket. However, a second hack followed shortly after, and even more customer funds were lost. In the end, the Bitcoinica story remained unresolved, and there has been no resolution to this very date. The fact that Bitcoinica was linked to Mt. Gox didn't help matters either.

September 2012 spelled the demise of bitcoin exchange BitFloor, during which 24,000 BTC were stolen by a hacker. To indicate how lackadaisical exchange security was at that time, the hacker managed to access an unencrypted backup of wallet keys. In the end, most of the lost customer funds were repaid, in U.S. dollars, not in bitcoin.

February 2013 is the darkest period in bitcoin history so far, as this was the time when the second Mt. Gox "hack" occurred, and the exchange shut down for good. Even though the company only held 2,000 BTC, users were owed 750,000 BTC in total. The investigation into the missing or stolen BTC is still ongoing at time of writing.

The list goes on and on. There were bitcoin exchange hacks in 2015 as well. There is a long way to go when it comes to creating a proper secure platform where users can trade and store their funds. But until that time comes, you are better off transferring funds out of an exchange at your earliest convenience.

Chapter 3

Bitcoin Pros and Cons

· ·

· ·

*E*verything has pros and cons, right? After all, without any cons, we'd get heavily addicted to the best things in life. A little bit of "con" can act as a balance if you understand it and may not hold you back if you're aware of it.

This chapter looks at both sides of the, um, bitcoin coin.

Adding Up the Pros of Bitcoin

Let's look on the bright side and start by considering the pros of bitcoin.

 These are my personal views about the positives of bitcoin. You may find other large plus points in using bitcoin. In fact, this chapter contains mostly opinion.

Financial freedom

Bitcoin offers its users many advantages, but perhaps the most important one is an unprecedented level of freedom. And that freedom comes in many different ways: financial freedom from not having to rely on existing infrastructure, for sure, but also the mental freedom of being in control of your own funds and technology.

Spending bitcoin for everyday goods and services — if it were to be adopted all around the world — would be as convenient, if not more so, than using a cash or card payment is right now. But it would also be vastly different, as you'd be in control of your own funds at any given time. No one could tell you where to store bitcoin, how to spend bitcoin, or what you could or could not do with it. The only limitations of financial freedom with bitcoin are the walls we create for ourselves. Wider adoption would see those walls come tumbling down.

Moving toward financial freedom

Banks and financial institutions have been slowly weaving a cocoon for us, tying us into using their services without any alternatives. And for most consumers, that works perfectly fine, as they are more than happy to stick to what they know. After all, if the system isn't broken, why try to fix it, right? But bitcoin does offer a viable alternative. But in order to achieve true financial freedom, we need to achieve a critical mass of bitcoin adoption first.

By *critical mass*, we mean the moment when bitcoin becomes a globally used form of technology and finance. Everyday consumers are still not aware of what bitcoin does, or how it can become a part of their everyday lives. Whether this is from a technological, financial, or ideological point of view depends on the user. Suffice to say that bitcoin is a very "niche" market right now, and although the community keeps growing every month, it still only represents a small portion of the world's population.

Buy a bitcoin, help civilization evolve

There are various ways as to how bitcoin and the underlying blockchain technology can help create a better financial ecosystem. If individuals in unbanked parts of the world could be paid in bitcoins and could use them to pay for their everyday needs, it would free and empower them. As a practical example, if you worked on a vineyard in sub-Saharan Africa and received payment in bitcoins, it would reduce the possibility of an immoral farmer paying you daily in an allowance of wine, and thus effectively enslaving you through alcoholism to that farmer.

These tools to take control of individual lives have yet to be developed. Some possibilities would be using the blockchain technology to manage contract negotiations and have the details stored in this transparent fashion. It could potentially be used in elections in a way that makes the voting process more transparent and less susceptible to corruption and election fraud. The potential positive benefits of real-world applications of the blockchain technology are really only limited by the imagination.

There are clearly significant commercial applications that will be developed. That said, the effects on the way that some of the less-privileged members of society should gain and benefit from enhanced personal freedoms, which in turn positively reinforce many aspects of their individual lives, is without question very exciting indeed!

Financial freedom through bitcoin won't be achieved simply by merchants becoming more willing to accept the digital currency as a payment, but also by consumers willing to use bitcoin. Plenty of places — both online and offline — allow you to use bitcoin to pay for goods and services, but true financial freedom would require more customers and consumers willing to use bitcoin over traditional payment methods.

Most of that stems from force of habit: The current financial infrastructure has created this for the consumer. Over the past 50 years, consumers went from being conditioned to use cash to pay for goods and services to using bank and credit cards. The next evolutionary step will be mobile payments, which are still linked to your bank account but in the future will no longer require you to carry either cash or a card on you.

Understanding our current lack of freedom

Another problem that bitcoin faces in terms of granting people financial freedom is that most consumers do not see the problem that is staring them right in the face: The current financial infrastructure is failing.

Printing ourselves into trouble

Picture this future scenario.

There's a total supply of 1 million U.S. dollars for the entire world, and the value drops to half of what it was. Every dollar is now worth 50 cents. The Federal Reserve decides to print an additional $1 million to stabilize the economy. You would then say that, because there's twice as much money, the value is restored to its previous level. But this is wrong.

Rather than every dollar having a value of 1, as it was at the beginning, there are now $2 million in circulation to achieve the value of $1 million. And with every dollar being worth 50 cents, $2 million adds up to $1 million again. Ouch!

But with double the money supply needed to achieve the same financial value, you are only worsening the problem, rather than solving it. Your original $1 million in circulation has not gained any value, and if the financial value were to devalue even further, the original supply would be worth even less than what it is today. In the end, a domino effect is created where layers of debt are put on top of layers of debt, until there is nothing left but empty promises. Double, triple, and quadruple ouch!

Should this cycle continue, a country could experience hyperinflation — as was the case in the German Weimar Republic in the 1920s or indeed as happened very recently in Zimbabwe from the mid-1990s until 2009. Now, though we must all assume that the central bankers are indeed acting in the interest of the common good, it's worth considering the potential negative effects.

If the U.S. Federal Reserve — or the European Central Bank for that matter — suddenly decides that more money needs to printed "to boost the economy," no one can stop them from doing so. If this were to happen — again — it would not solve the existing problem of fiat currencies dropping in value, but would instead increase the amount of debt. And the everyday consumer will pick up the bill for that debt, because we're the ones empowering these centralized bodies to make the situation even worse.

Printing additional money means more money is in circulation, which is true. But only so much value may be linked to the existing money supply, and that additional money only further devalues the existing supply. It's a vicious circle, and one that bitcoin sits outside of. See the sidebar "Printing ourselves into trouble" for a nightmare scenario that could well come true.

Checking out the difference between bitcoin and currency freedom

The nightmare scenario created in the sidebar "Printing ourselves into trouble" brings us to one of the major differences between bitcoin and fiat currency, especially in terms of financial freedom.

The fiat currency you have in your wallet or in your bank account represents a certain value. For example, a 20 euro bill is "worth" 20 EUR. Or that is what the financial institutions tell you anyway, as there is no way for the everyday consumer to verify how much their piece of paper is actually worth.

With bitcoin, the free market determines the price of a bitcoin, or even smallest divisible unit, called a *satoshi*. If the free market — which is made up by all of the bitcoin users around the world — decides that the new bitcoin price should not be U.S. $250, but U.S. $10,000, no central authority can say this cannot happen. Bitcoin is one of the very few transportable and borderless digital currencies that can both lose value — like fiat currency — but also gain value, like precious metals.

Granted, the bitcoin price is currently denominated in various local currencies, which is also a positive thing. Even though bitcoin itself is a borderless payment method to send and receive money, it still has to be converted to fiat currency in most countries before it becomes usable. This level of financial freedom allows anyone in the world to send value to anyone else on this planet, and they can convert it to fiat currency or store it in BTC, depending on their preferences.

Bitcoin removes the need for remittance services such as MoneyGram and Western Union, which not only charge high fees, but also require personal information and verification every time you send or receive a payment. Bitcoin requires no verification of identity, giving users a level of privacy protection they are not accustomed to, either through the use of cash or banking services.

Freeing your mind

On a mental level, being free from all of the obstacles put along our way by traditional financial infrastructures is a moment of sweet liberty. In fact, you have to experience it for yourself before you can even believe it. And there are many options at your disposal to experience that freedom, ranging from paying everyday bills in bitcoin, to receiving (part of) your wages in bitcoin. All the necessary tools to cut out the middleman — banks and like-minded institutions — are at your disposal and undergoing continuous development to improve the service they offer.

The same can be said for the ideological freedom associated with bitcoin. Even by using bitcoin as an everyday consumer, you are actively helping build and strengthen the bitcoin network. And with more people using digital currency, there's more interest from merchants, institutions, governments, and companies, which in turn leads to further improvements to the way in which bitcoin operates and functions — collectively known as the *bitcoin protocol.* And that future development will help create a better world for everyone. Call it a butterfly effect if you will, but the best way to support bitcoin is by being an active member of the network and the ever-growing community.

Security

When it comes to security, bitcoin generates a lot of discussion. This is because the same aspects that give bitcoin its level of freedom also create a security concern for people. And this is a fair point, as there are security risks associated with any financial vehicle, including bitcoin.

Bitcoin is not subject to the desires and whims of central bankers who may want to devalue their currency in order for their economy to become more competitive, for example. Thus, in pure financial terms, bitcoin potentially offers a more secure and robust system in its own right compared to traditional financial institutions. Assuming that, with time, there is enough liquidity and a sufficient volume of trading within the bitcoin ecosystem, it should be the case that the market truly decides the value of bitcoin and that no institution or group of traders for instance should be able to influence the prices significantly. Services associated with bitcoin are always on the lookout for security improvements, and future implementations of blockchain technology will only increase the overall network security.

Most individuals want to have as much control as possible over their finances, and the same is true of bitcoin users. And if the devices you do your banking on are not properly secured, no one will bail you out if you lose your money. In the case of bitcoin, security starts with users themselves, rather than signing up for a service and trusting the service with their money. Keep in mind such services exist in the world of bitcoin as well, but they were never intended to be used in that manner. Remember that bitcoin is a decentralized system, and this applies to security too — you need to be aware and take control of this from the very start.

From a technological point of view, the blockchain technology (covered in Chapter 7) that powers the bitcoin network is applicable to many different aspects of life. Most of these implementations will include a higher level of security than we are using now, and we have only just begun to uncover the potential of blockchain technology. A simple example of how blockchain technology could improve the current security features we use on a daily basis comes in the form of *passwordless login*. To access most types of services or platforms, such as e-mail, you traditionally need to enter a username and a password. Blockchain technology could make the system of usernames and passwords redundant by implementing a login system linked to the blockchain and your bitcoin wallet address. No more forgotten passwords for bitcoin users!

Beyond identity security, bitcoin is helpful to security in other ways too. Counterfeit goods are a huge thorn in the side of governments all around the world. Whether in the form of clothing, software piracy, or even medicine, people are losing money and getting hurt because of this criminal activity. With blockchain technology, we can track the manufacturing process of every item we purchase and verify whether or not it is genuine. Whether governments in all parts of the world would be keen to roll out such a scheme remains to be seen — let's just say that some may be more willing than others.

The underlying technology of the bitcoin network allows us to discover and implement many new security features which we could have only dreamed of a decade ago. But it will take time before we can harness that technological advancement, and we need more active developers looking into the possibilities. The bitcoin network is only as strong and secure as the people — both general users and developers — who are supporting it. It will require patience.

Removing fraud

One of the biggest flaws in the current financial infrastructure is the risk of fraud and chargebacks.

Fraud comes in many forms, ranging from counterfeit cash bills to stolen credit cards, hacked PayPal accounts, and breached bank accounts. But there is also fraud on the receiving end, as some payment methods do not allow you to receive a refund.

Trusting no one

If you want to buy something online on a platform like eBay or even a regular web shop, the only likely payment options are credit cards, PayPal, or wire transfer. Choosing a wire transfer would be the worst possible option in this case, as wire transfers are nonrefundable.

Should you send money to the bank account of the company running the web shop? You would be trusting them to be honest, acknowledge they received the funds, and ship your goods. But there is no way to ensure they will ever do so. And if they don't, you have no way to claim your money back, even though you are technically "protected" by your financial institution. Crazy, eh?

Using PayPal is not the safest option either. PayPal protects the seller in most cases, even though it advertises "Buyer Protection." Fraud from either party is possible, because the seller can receive money and never ship the goods, or the buyer can receive the goods, claim they never received them, and ask for a refund anyway. If you pay for an item and never receive it, you can open a dispute; but if the seller can provide a tracking number — even if they shipped an empty box — there is not much else a buyer can do.

Which brings us to the most insecure payment method to ever be accepted by both online and physical stores: credit cards. A credit card is a piece of plastic with a magnetic code that contains a lot of confidential personal information, such as your card number, expiration date, CVV code, and even the pin code of your card. In some cases, all that information is stored on the chip on your credit card.

The major problem with credit cards is that you have to physically hand over the card or card details in order to make a payment. Even though more countries will let you insert the card into a card reader, they will still take out the card and check your signature. And you usually need to verify that signature by either signing the receipt or showing them a government-issued ID card. Neither method is very safe and both can be seen as breaches of user privacy.

. . . apart from bitcoin

A BTC transaction can't be reversed. Once the funds have been sent to a different address — even if it is still waiting for network confirmations — you can't get your money back. This is also one of the downsides about being in control of your own finances again: There is no one to bail you out if things go awry.

Always check the payment details before executing a transaction.

That being said, bitcoin's non-reversible aspect is a blessing for merchants who are otherwise at the mercy of traditional financial institutions. As soon as a bitcoin payment is made, the merchant can fulfill the order without having to worry about a potential chargeback or refund. Bitcoin does allow for merchants to refund an order in case of damaged goods, as they have the bitcoin address where the money was sent from.

Rather than relying on a credit card company or bank to process the refund, merchants can take care of this process on their own. Plus, bitcoin transactions are credited and debited a lot faster than traditional payment methods, which is beneficial to both buyer and seller in the long run.

Bitcoin does a lot to prevent fraud for the merchant and the customer in the regular financial process. But if a user's wallet gets breached and coins are stolen, there is very little that can be done to prevent those stolen funds from being spent by the thief. Though such an event is technically not fraud, the merchant could be on the receiving end of fraudulently acquired coins — not that that will be visible, nor should it usually be of much concern to the merchant, as they received funds from a user and completed an order. That said, unlike with a fiat currency, there is no central regulator, and thus once again end-users need to assume responsibility for their own security.

Transparency

The biggest advantage presented by bitcoin — or to be more precise, the underlying blockchain technology (see Chapter 7) — comes in the form of creating a completely transparent trading system.

For those individuals and businesses who may want to avoid transparency — such as, for instance, in the non-declaration of various taxes, the transparency of bitcoin may be an issue. However, not only does the blockchain act as a public ledger for every financial transaction on the bitcoin network, it can also be adapted to suit other needs such as file storage, property ownership, trading of assets, or even verifying the manufacturing process of medicine. The possibilities are really only limited to the bounds of human ingenuity.

The major focus of bitcoin and blockchain technology has always been in terms of finances. And although bitcoin lets you send money to anyone else in the world at little to no cost — and gives you the ability to track this payment to the recipient — that may not be ideal for everyone. This is why it is so important to keep in mind that bitcoin is much more than a payment method. For example, you can put the ownership of your car on the blockchain and have it time-stamped by the network when the block associated with your data is confirmed. If you ever sell that car, you can digitally transfer its ownership by sending it to anyone else on the bitcoin blockchain. And once that transfer has completed and confirmed on the network, the new owner can officially lay claim to that car. No paperwork needed — just the exchange of keys and the sending of the digital asset which represents the car.

Not every consumer wants to see his or her financial details broadcasted on a public ledger for anyone to see. That is completely understandable, but you have to keep in mind that everyone is pseudonymous on the bitcoin network — there's no reason to think that anyone else will find out who are you if you don't want them to. Your *wallet address* is what links the transaction, but there is no name or physical location attached to the address itself.

That being said, the current financial infrastructure offers no oversight as to how bitcoin's stored value is being used. The funds you keep in a savings account are there for you to see, represented by a list of digits in terms of what the bank owes you. But everyone knows banks are using your money to create more money, though you have no idea how that is happening. All you know is that banks are playing with your money, and if they lose too much of it, they need to be bailed out by the government. Or to be more precise: Everyday consumers need to bail out the banks because they lost the money we let them safeguard for us.

The transparent nature of bitcoin and blockchain technology is beneficial in so many ways to so many people. With more and more companies and developers focusing on additional uses for the blockchain outside of the financial space, you never know what might be in store next. And if you have a good idea, why not join in, start using bitcoin, and see where it leads?

Low fees

If there's one thing about bitcoin that improves finances for people all around the world, it is that as a digital currency, bitcoin transactions invoke very low — or non-existent — fees to move money across borders. Hooray! This flies in the face of traditional financial infrastructure, which charges fees of up to $50 for international wire transfers, or remittance solutions such as Western Union, whose fee structure may amount to more than that depending on the amount to be sent and the location of the receiver.

You could argue that precious metals can be used as a way to transfer value across borders as well. And although there is merit to that statement, moving gold or silver around incurs other fees in terms of logistics, which usually end up more costly than the afore-mentioned methods. And exactly how many gold bars do you have tucked away behind the sofa?

And this is where bitcoin is making a global impression, by taking on the current remittance market. Especially in countries where it is difficult — or sometimes even impossible — to get a bank account or credit card, bitcoin can make a large impact in provid-ing citizens with an alternate form of payment that can be con-verted into any global currency.

Several companies are already competing in this market, targeting areas such as Africa and the Philippines. So far, these services are successful on a smaller scale, but they will likely be expanding at an exponential pace in the future once word gets out from local communities. And there are plenty of improvements to make to this system in the future, as we are only just learning the potential of blockchain technology.

The same principle of low fees applies to those who are receiving bitcoin, as any transaction fee associated with the transfer is paid by the sender. This opens up a lot of ways for companies to cut down on overhead costs whenever they have to pay their employees, especially remote workers in a different country. Plus it also removes any delays in payments that can otherwise take up to several weeks to clear.

Subtracting the Cons of Bitcoin

Bitcoin is great! Yeah, okay, we all know that already. We hope you're feeling pretty sold on the concept right now. But hold onto your hat for just one moment: In the interest of fair play, we want to highlight a few potential downsides.

Awareness and understanding

Talk to the average Joe on the street about bitcoin, and you'll probably receive one of two possible responses:

✔ They've heard of bitcoin because of Silk Road, Mt. Gox, or other type of scam associated with this disruptive currency.

These types of bitcoin stories have been picked up by main-stream media all over the world.

✔ They've not heard of it or they know a few things but cannot put the whole concept and ideology together. Lack of main-stream exposure is one of the issues that has been plaguing bitcoin for quite some time now; its PR image caters to tech-savvy people.

Raising bitcoin's profile

In fairness to the average Joe, the entire bitcoin concept is fairly technical, as most of the focus revolves around blockchain technology. But you don't need to know every nook and cranny about bitcoin in order to use it. Setting up a bitcoin wallet requires the installation of software on a computer or an app on a mobile device. There's nothing else to it. (Want me to prove it? Head over to Chapter 2 for advice on setting up your wallet.)

Still, there are a ton of people out there who have never heard of bitcoin. And even if they have — in one way or another — they may not have any interest in it. As a result, there is an educational problem with bitcoin, which causes analysts to call the technology "far ahead of its time." The more bitcoin enthusiasts can convince others to use it for their transactions with us, the more it will grow, and the more common knowledge of bitcoin will be.

As long as there are no more educational efforts focusing on bit-coin on a consumer level, it will never gain mainstream adoption. The technology side is pretty well covered for now, with tons of companies working on various implementations. The time has come to educate the average people on the street on the benefits of bitcoin and why it is in their best interest to get involved. We like to think that's where this book comes in. Share it widely!

Meeting up with bitcoin people

If you can convince someone to try bitcoin, a domino effect often follows. Spreading the word about bitcoin on a level people can understand, comprehend, and tell to others is the key to gaining mass adoption in the future. All hail, bitcoin!

Unfortunately, information on bitcoin through conversation or presentation is not that easy to come by. There are several bitcoin conferences around the world every year, but ticket prices are too high for the average person to attend. Most of the sessions are later posted online, such as on YouTube later on though, which is a good thing. Keep your eyes peeled in the online community for further news.

Luckily, there are still local bitcoin meetup groups all around the world. These kinds of meetups are a great way to get to know people with a passion for bitcoin in or nearby a major city in your area. Plus, bitcoin meetups are free to attend as well. You can find out more about your local bitcoin group by heading over to www. meetup.com and typing **bitcoin** into the search box. And even if there's no bitcoin meetup in your area, no one's stopping you from organizing such an event yourself. It doesn't cost any money, and most people prefer to meet up in a public place, such as a bar or restaurant where everyone can pay separately. Even if that place does not accept bitcoin, people will be more than happy to meet up.

One of the things a lot of people really like about bitcoin meetups is that you can attend any of these events without any prior knowledge about bitcoin. And one of the greatest moments during meetups happens when you can inform someone about all of the wonders digital currency and blockchain technology can help us achieve. Keep in mind these explanations do not have to be technical at all for people to understand.

Bitcoin can unite people from all different aspects of life, and once you find some common ground, it becomes easy to strike up a conversation. Once you find yourself in a position where you feel you have a natural way of explaining bitcoin and digital currency to people, you can always consider giving presentations on the subject.

There are usually plenty of opportunities to become a speaker. Granted, this is not something just anyone can do, as you have to feel comfortable speaking for larger audiences. At bitcoin meetups, these crowds are anywhere from 5 to 150 people, whereas conferences usually draw around 300–500 people.

What might be even more important than just giving a presentation is finding ways to engage your audience. This is the same for a one-to-one conversation as it is when addressing multiple people. Make sure they can interact with you, rather than just sit around and listen.

Once people become interested in the concept of bitcoin, they automatically want to learn more on the subject and the underlying technology. There is so much to tell about bitcoin without even involving words like "blockchain" or "technology." Just describe bitcoin for what it stands for, rather than what it is trying to achieve right now.

Trust

One of the core elements of any kind of payment technology is trust. If you don't trust your bank, you will never use a bank account or a debit or credit card. You'll keep your money in cash in a drawer somewhere. The same can be said for bitcoin: If you don't trust it, you will likely stick with the financial infrastructure you are used to. "The devil you know" is quite an appropriate saying in that regard. Check out the nearby sidebar on trusting modern tech for a mind-changing viewpoint.

 Given the number of headlines concerning bitcoin and scams, hacks, illegitimate services, and whatnot, there is a huge trust issue bitcoin needs to overcome. Rather than trusting the economic value of a bitcoin individually, it is more important to put your trust in the entire bitcoin network. That includes all associated services, companies, mining pools, and users in existence today, plus the ones that will be joining the network in the future.

Bitcoin is still in its very early stages. It has been around for a little over six years at the time of writing. As is the case with any form of payment method, adoption is slow and faces a lot of adversity and scrutiny from competitors. One thing people tend to forget is that bitcoin is not necessarily here to replace the current payment methods, but to show how things can be done differently in a more transparent manner.

You need to ask yourself the following question: "Do I trust the current payment infrastructure enough to keep my data safe at all times, not give it to third parties and protect me from financial harm?" If the answer to that question is not a resolute yes, then bitcoin is definitely worth checking out.

Even though most finances are currently being controlled by financial institutions who have failed customers time and again, we still trust them with our money. The reason for that is simple: It is convenient to use a bank account and bank card for storing and transferring money. Because that is how we were taught to use it. It's also true to say that banks have a virtual monopoly on what they do in providing financial services, and alternatives have historically been few and far between.

These days, there seems to be a shift in consumerism, as traditional financial institutions want to dictate how we can spend money, and more importantly, how much we can spend. In most countries, banks limit the maximum amount of money you can withdraw from an ATM to 500 euros or $750.

Granted, in the Western world, consumers have other options to pay for goods and services. Bank cards, credit cards, and even bank transfers are frequently used to pay for just about anything, and cash is slowly becoming obsolete. But what if banks decide to limit the funds you can spend by using any of those other payments as well?

Traditional financial institutions want to hold on to any funds you deposit as long as possible, so they can loan the money to other service providers and accumulate interest on it. This is one of the reasons why wire transfers take several days to reach their destination, as every bank wants to take a cut of the fees for as long as they possibly can. Other reasons include the inherent slowness of the banking clearing platforms such as the SWIFT network. Although the pan-European SEPA (Single Euro Payments Area) platform has facilitated quicker wire transfers within European countries, the actual performance and functionality may rely on how the system has been implemented by individual banks.

Not that there is anything wrong with that — it's a business model like any other. That said, the customer is the victim of these delays, because late payments invoke more fees from the company waiting for its money. There are ways to speed up the process, but financial infrastructures are sticking to their old methods.

Or to be more precise, there is one way to change that system, and that is by uniting and demanding change. Wouldn't you like to see your money stored on a public ledger, which you can check at all times and send to anyone in the world without delays or transaction costs? If the answer is yes, then bitcoin is worth checking out.

No one is saying you need to put your full trust in bitcoin from the start, as there is a lot of information to sift through. But if you are willing to keep an open mind to what bitcoin stands for and the point it is trying to get across, you can make a weighted decision on whether or not to put your trust in digital currencies.

Trusting modern technology

Trust is something that is easily given by consumers these days. We blindly trust most of the services we use on a daily basis. Social media platforms such as Facebook, Twitter, and Instagram hold a lot of our valuable data, all of which we are more than happy to give to them. Why? Because we trust them enough with our data so that we can conveniently share it with friends and family.

But hardly anyone realizes what these companies can do with our data. When signing up for an account on any of these services, we accept their terms and conditions. And those terms and conditions usually state that they can share the data with third parties for advertising and other purposes.

Yet many who blindly trust Google, Apple, Facebook, and others end up taking a negative stance toward bitcoin. That is the major difference between services we use that do not touch our finances, compared to services that are disrupting the financial world. Human nature makes us wary of everything that is new and brings change, as we do not like to change things all that much.

Now if the banks themselves all had a blockchain-based transactional system, transfers anywhere within that network would be done almost instantaneously, with funds available to spend shortly thereafter. With such a system in place, there's no reason why a Nigerian migrant worker based in the UK couldn't send his family back in his home country money within a couple minutes — now wouldn't that be something!

Risk and volatility

Bitcoin is a financial tool that carries risks just like any other payment method or currency does. However, with bitcoin, those risks are slightly different from traditional currencies and payments. Part of that comes in the form of a rather volatile price, but then again, any local currency fluctuates on a daily basis.

Bitcoin and the underlying blockchain technology reduce a lot of the risks presented by traditional payment methods. There are no chargebacks, fraud is tough due to transparency, and the transaction fees are very low compared to credit cards, wire transfers, or remittance services.

That's not to say that there are no risks attached to bitcoin either though. It's a new breed of technology which is part ideology and part payment method. The technology is still under development as we speak. We are still discovering potential use cases for blockchain technology. So if you're planning to invest in bitcoin from a technological development point of view, there is always risk involved. Even the best solutions and implementations may not be viable in the end, if nobody adopts them.

But there is a flipside to that story as well. Blockchain technology development shows lots of room for growth and creates jobs in the long run. Every new technological discovery needs people who can implement and maintain this new advancement, and preferably in a user-friendly way.

From a technological standpoint, there is hardly any risk when investing in bitcoin itself. Investing in a company that is working on this new technology is a different matter altogether, but that principle is the same for any company you want to invest in. Bitcoin company investments are not inherently riskier than investing in any other startup company.

When it comes to speculating on the bitcoin price however, the story is a bit different. If you look at bitcoin from the perspective of an investment vehicle that will likely gain value, there are quite a few risks attached. Speculating on price volatility is never a good idea, and bitcoin is proving to be rather volatile on a daily basis.

Ever since its inception, economists and investors have been keeping a close eye on the bitcoin price. What started out as a worthless digital token quickly rose to something that actually held
value, once the U.S. $1 mark was reached. And even though the
price continued to rise and fall until its peak of over $1,100 in 2013,
many people still viewed it as fake Internet money.

To this day, bitcoin is often referred to as just that: "fake internet
money." Meanwhile, bitcoin has been making waves in the financial
world. Investors from all over have been buying up bitcoin, as they
feel BTC is a safer method of storing and transferring value compared to precious metals or traditional payment methods.

Limited use (for now)

Bitcoin cannot be used for every aspect of our daily lives just yet,
even though you can pay with BTC for virtually anything in-store
or online. On top of that, you can even pay regular bills in bitcoin
using a third-party service. But none of that was the intended use
envisioned for bitcoin and blockchain technology: The main objec-
tive was to cut out the middleman.

It will take a few more years — at least — until merchants start
pricing their goods and services in BTC value rather than using the
conversion from a major currency. But before that can happen, bitcoin needs to be adopted by the mainstream consumer, not just an
"inner circle" of enthusiasts. And bitcoin can only gain mass adoption once we get more educational efforts underway in all regions
of the world. Unfortunately, most of these education efforts are
U.S.-oriented, where bitcoin will most likely not be making an
impact in the immediate future.

Key areas and emerging markets such as Africa, Asia, and even
Australia have been overlooked in our opinion. Even though
Australia may be an odd name on that shortlist, it is an interesting
area for digital currency regardless. Asia and Africa are obvious
choices, due to their remittance market potential, being underbanked, and technological prowess.

Despite all of that, bitcoin is usable as a payment method for virtually anything, though you may have to jump through some hoops.
Bitcoin debit cards are proving to be a great example, as they
allow you to spend BTC wherever major credit cards are accepted.
However, that will not push merchants to accept bitcoin all of a
sudden, as it is just a regular card transaction to them.

And paying bills with bitcoin is possible as well, even though
those services are limited to SEPA zones only for the time being.

Once again, this will not push companies to accept bitcoin all of a sudden, as they receive a regular bank transfer like they always have done. But both of these examples serve a different purpose.

SEPA zones are European countries where the SEPA protocol is used by banks and financial institutions. SEPA allows citizens to send bank transfers, denominated in euros, to other countries using the euro in a short span of time (usually one to two business days).

SEPA is a forerunner of bitcoin — a case that has the potential to change the financial system as we know it. Whereas the blockchain technology is still being fine-tuned — and will take many more years — bitcoin can easily be converted to a different fiat currency and used to pay for goods and services.

With mobile payments becoming more widespread, bitcoin is a very strong contender. In fact, mobile bitcoin wallets were available even before most financial institutions unveiled their mobile apps. And most of these wallets have been improved over the past few years, making the transfer of bitcoin as easy as scanning a QR code with your mobile device's camera.

Whatever the future may hold, odds are bitcoin, or at least its blockchain technology, will play a major role in it. If things go according to plan, both the blockchain and bitcoin will be the most commonly used methods to transfer money across borders at zero fees. In fact, bitcoin may become the best form of money ever invented.

Chapter 4

Making Money with Bitcoin

*T*his chapter explains the various methods you can use to make money with bitcoin. Investing in bitcoin is the most obvious answer, but there are other ways at your disposal as well. Not all of these methods cost very much money either, so read through and see which method suits you best.

Mining Bitcoins

Bitcoin mining is a slightly misleading name. No one swings a pick-axe into rough stones in order to find additional bitcoins (at least, I *hope* no one is trying that). Bitcoin mining actually means adding more bitcoins to the digital currency ecosystem.

There will be a total of 21 million bitcoin in circulation by 2140, and there are roughly 15 million in existence at the time of this writing.

How bitcoin mining works

So, how do new bitcoins come into existence? All the additional bitcoins have to be generated through a computational process called *mining*. You do it by letting your computer hardware calculate complex mathematical equations, which can be done at any given time of the day. Doing so enables you to become an integral part of the bitcoin network, not only by securing the network through your dedicated hardware, but also by generating more coins to put into circulation.

There are certain similarities to how other resources — such as gold — are mined: The available supply is slowly increased as more is being put into the mining process. That said, the way bitcoins are mined is by solving complex computational problems, which require more resources as time progresses.

To ensure that no more coins are generated every day than originally intended, the mining process is linked to a *difficulty rating*. This rating goes up as more computational power joins the bitcoin network, and decreases when there are fewer miners competing for network blocks.

A short history of bitcoin mining

Over the years, bitcoin mining has seen a tremendous evolution in terms of the required hardware to mine bitcoins. Very little hardware was required when bitcoin launched in 2009, as there was little to no interest in the project. But as more and more people caught wind of bitcoin and joined the network, the computational power increased exponentially. The *mining difficulty parameter* (which determines how much computation power is required to solve the mathematical equations associated with generating bitcoins) adjusted accordingly, in order to make sure new blocks on the bitcoin network were still ten minutes apart. The reason for keeping bitcoin blocks ten minutes apart is to collect as many broadcasted bitcoin transactions into one block and validate these transactions at the same time.

In 2009, the first versions of the bitcoin client had a built-in process that would let anyone running the software mine bitcoin with their computer's central processing unit (CPU) — the main processor in a computer. Because every computer has a CPU, and only a handful of people were mining bitcoins at that time, there was very little competition. In fact, most of the coins in the first few months were mined by Satoshi Nakamoto, who also gave away some coins to other people in order to allow testing of the bitcoin network.

It didn't take long for one of the miners to figure out that the mining feature could be adapted to use a graphics processing unit (GPU), rather than just a CPU. Because a GPU — also called a video card — is specifically designed to solve complex mathematical tasks, it is able to mine bitcoin more efficiently than a CPU. However, that performance is offset by a large increase in electricity use, as GPUs draw a lot more power from the wall compared to CPUs. This change was the first chapter in a long and storied bitcoin mining arms race.

Developers and engineers started tinkering around with the idea of creating a new piece of hardware that mined much faster and more efficiently than GPUs and CPUs. Field Programmable Gate Arrays (FPGAs) saw the light of day a few years ago, and they outperformed CPU mining by quite a margin. Furthermore, any FPGA could mine nearly as fast as a GPU available at that time — while using far less electricity to complete the task of mining bitcoins.

When reading up on bitcoin mining these days, one term people often come across is *ASIC,* which stands for *application-specific integrated circuit.* This is a microchip designed specifically to mine bitcoin. The first bitcoin ASICs started hitting the street in early 2013, and they outperformed GPU and FPGA mining by such a margin that miners scrambled to get their hands on one of these shiny machines. But ASICs have a major downside as well: They are very power hungry, they make a lot of noise, and they generate a ton of heat. On the flipside, a bitcoin ASIC miner is vastly superior to any other type of hardware in existence today and remains quite costly in some cases.

As these new devices started popping up, the need for electricity increased exponentially. As a result, mining bitcoins is extremely unprofitable in most parts of the world, unless you have access to cheap or free electricity. In most cases, the investment cost of bitcoin hardware, combined with the electricity costs, make it impossible to make a profit by mining at home. But there is a solution to that problem: Bitcoin *cloud mining* lets you mine bitcoin by purchasing mining power from a machine hosted in a different part of the world.

Cloud mining has become somewhat popular in recent years. It allows you to mine without needing to buy and/or host the hardware yourself. Most bitcoin cloud mining providers charge a daily or monthly fee to cover electricity costs. Cloud mining allows a user to start earning money directly, rather than waiting on the delivery of some fancy machine. Chapter 11 talks more about cloud mining.

In the future, as with all computer advancements, microchips will be made smaller without sacrificing computational power. And with smaller chips, more of them can be fitted onto a board, increasing the machine's overall mining power. Engineers are trying to reduce the energy use of these microchips too. Making mining more energy efficient could lead to more profitability in additional parts of the world.

Trading Bitcoins

Trading bitcoins is one of the easiest and most lucrative ways of making money with digital currency. The bitcoin price is volatile, which means it goes up and down on a regular basis. Experienced traders can profit by predicting price increases or decreases.

Successful bitcoin trades can earn you a decent amount of money over time, but be aware that things can go the other way as well. Always trade at your own risk, and only use money you can afford to lose.

Day trading versus fiat

Day trading is buying and selling financial instruments — such as bitcoin — within the same trading day. *Fiat currency* refers to a national government's legal tender.

Using bitcoin allows you to trade in several different ways. The most obvious way of trading is exchanging bitcoins to and from any of the local currencies it can be traded against. In most cases, people decide to go after the major fiat currency markets because they generate a lot more trading volume compared to smaller currencies. Hence, the biggest fiat trading market is China, where BTC is traded against Chinese yuan (CNY). Depending on where you live, you may or may not have easy access to CNY for trading purposes. However, a quick call or trip to your local bank may provide you with some very useful information on how to obtain Chinese yuan and at which exchange rate — assuming you are planning to go through with playing the Chinese bitcoin day-trading market.

Other major currencies can be easily converted to and from bitcoin as well, thanks to the multiple exchanges supporting these currencies; at the time of writing, these currencies include the following:

- British pounds
- Canadian dollars
- Euros
- Russian rubles
- U.S. dollars

If you already own bitcoin, there is no need to obtain any type of fiat currency prior to starting your day-trading experience. Transfer over the bitcoin balance you want to play around with to your favorite exchange and start trading against the fiat currency of your choice. Bitcoin is well known for its volatile nature, so there are gains and losses to be made each and every day. Sometimes those losses or gains will be big, whereas other times they may not be. Alas, that is the life of day trading.

Still other options, besides buying and selling Bitcoin directly, allow you to speculate on the bitcoin/fiat currency markets. Several trading platforms exist that let you speculate on the increase or decrease in bitcoin price versus a certain market — and they even accept bitcoin as payment. These include:

- ✔ Vaultoro (`https://vaultoro.com`), a bitcoin/gold exchange

- ✔ Kraken Bitcoin Exchange against Fiat (`http://kraken.com`)

- ✔ Plus500 (`www.plus500.com`)

- ✔ Avatrade (`www.avatrade.com`)

- ✔ Etoro (`www.etoro.com`)

Even though quite a few merchants accept bitcoin payments, nearly all of the funds are converted to fiat currency directly. This is done in order to protect the merchant from any bitcoin price volatility that may occur, which is one of the reasons why so many shopkeepers are happy to join the digital currency train.

On the other hand, these conversions from bitcoin to fiat currency also create a side effect, as there will be sell pressure across the major exchanges. Bitcoin payment processors need to liquidate those bitcoin payments as soon as possible to pay the right amount to the merchant. As a result, there can be a few hefty BTC sell orders going through at certain times, which create a perfect opportunity to scoop up some slightly cheaper bitcoins.

It has to be said, however, that speculating on the bitcoin price is certainly not for the faint-hearted and should be approached with a great deal of caution. Granted, the traditional factors influencing fiat currency also influence the bitcoin price in some way; of more danger is the way in which a new scam, or a major vote of confidence for or against bitcoin, can both shake up the price quite a bit. Yet there is not always a clear reason for a bitcoin price change either, as these things just happen.

Day trading versus altcoins

Okay, so you have an idea of what day trading is from the previous section (if you skipped it, flick back to get a definition). Let me introduce *altcoins* — also known as alternative currencies. These are bitcoin clones, bitcoin rivals (boo, hiss!). By the time you're reading this book, there will be well over 4,000 different altcoins in existence.

If you do not like to trade or speculate on the bitcoin against fiat currency markets, you could trade against altcoins instead. Altcoins seek to improve on the ideas bitcoin represents. Some people feel the need for more anonymity, whereas other developers want to explore the boundaries of the underlying blockchain technology. Rather than submitting their ideas to the bitcoin developers, they use the bitcoin code, change the name, make some minor tweaks, and launch it as a brand new digital currency.

 Over the years, only a dozen or so altcoins have managed to stay relevant over time, mostly thanks to a strong community and the integration of some unique features that have not made it to bitcoin core (yet). Nevertheless, none of these altcoin communities is as large or as supportive as the bitcoin community. But that doesn't mean there is no speculation going in the altcoin scene either. And this is why so many day traders prefer to speculate on the altcoin markets, as there is a lot of room for quick profits and quick losses.

Most altcoins are created by *pump-and-dump* groups. What this means is that developers create a lot of hype for their coin and promise unique and interesting features. As people find out about these promises, they are more eager to buy coins at a low price, which in turn pushes the price upward. A few altcoins that have people who are actively working hard outside of pump-and-dump groups include Litecoin, CasinoCoin, and Guldencoin.

 Rather than pushing up the price by buying coins, some altcoin developers encourage community members to put down a lot of money for a valueless altcoin. And once the price is high enough, these developers cash out, take their money, and work on a new coin for next week.

 There are many altcoins to go around, and most of them will never serve an actual purpose. However, if you can catch a few cheap coins before the price increases, there is a nice amount of profit to be made. Never become too greedy though, as prices can plummet even faster than they rise.

Crowdfunding with Bitcoin

Rather than relying on one investor, or one major source of funding, a crowdfunding campaign allows you to decentralize the funding process by acquiring backers and supporters to provide money up front. By accepting bitcoin as a payment method for your campaign, you can decentralize things even further and reach a global audience.

Bitcoin provides businesses and individuals with a powerful tool to raise funds for an upcoming or existing project. Considering the fact that bitcoin is not taxable in most countries, many people view it as a safe haven for "tax-free" funding.

When you convert the raised funds to fiat currency, you may be taxed on them, depending on the amount you receive.

When crowdfunding, never list a fake project or claim to do something with the money you never intend to fulfill. Even though bitcoin is a non-reversible payment method, people will hunt you down if you try to run off with their money.

Luckily for bitcoin enthusiasts, most crowdfunding projects so far have been legitimate, and most have delivered on their promises as well. Depending on what type of project you list, it may take additional time to reach your goals, especially if it involves blockchain technology development.

But not every project is using crowdfunding platforms for the right reasons. Some people view crowdfunding as a way to get some funds quickly, without ever having to pay it back. Even though most platforms implement security against misuse, there is always a minor chance of a project not delivering on the promises made. But that has nothing to do with bitcoin per se — it can happen with any type of crowdfunding campaign. Simply look at how many people backed projects in Kickstarter and never received the item for which they pledged a certain amount. Check out www. kickstarter.com/help/stats for more.

Whenever you help crowdfund a bitcoin project, always determine whether you are entitled to some form of reward. Crowdfunding is not the same as buying a share of a company or product at a cheaper rate. It simply means you're willing to spend money in order to make someone's dream come true, which may or may not include a reward. However, you should not partake in a crowdfunding campaign just for the reward. That's not why this system was invented in the first place.

Understanding ICOs and IPOs

Initial coin offerings (ICOs) and *initial public offerings* (IPOs) are not droids from *Star Wars*. They're financial terms:

- ✔ **ICO:** Potential investors are given the chance to purchase a part of the altcoin's total supply before the mining process begins. Most investors do so in the hopes of seeing the price per coin increase in the near future.

- ✔ **IPO:** An IPO takes place when a bitcoin or altcoin company or project hopes to raise additional funds for its operations. Investors receive a share in said company and earn interest, paid out in recurring dividends.

Both terms carry a slightly negative connotation in the world of bitcoin crowdfunding, because multiple false promises and scam projects have been associated with ICO and IPO promises. That said, both are being used for legitimate purposes as well.

For example, whenever you're planning to create a new use case for blockchain technology which uses its own *token* (another word for coin), you are effectively holding an ICO. Per certain amount invested, the user will receive X amount of tokens in return to use on the new platform once it has been launched. You are effectively offering your backers a tangible reward, even though it may not come in a physical form. Whether these digital tokens will gain value over time completely depends on the success of your project. But you are also incentivizing backers to spread the word about your crowdfunding campaign, which will go a long way in terms of developing a successful platform.

You don't have to hand out digital tokens for people who want to back your project. However, investors — both small and large — like nothing more than some sort of return on investment, preferably sooner rather than later. Using an ICO/IPO may help you in that regard, entirely depending on the magnitude of your project and what it entails exactly.

 You're putting additional stress on yourself whenever you're creating — or investing in — a project that involves an ICO or IPO. As an investor, you will need to keep track of the progress and make sure you're given the coins you have paid for. And as a developer or project creator, you have responsibilities to live up to, including the distribution of these digital assets to the right people.

Creating a crowdfunding campaign with an IPO/ICO generates both excitement and expectations at the same time. Although people will see the value of your project, they are also speculating that the digital asset price will increase once your project goes live. And if there is one thing that can be said for people who trust you with their money, it's that they're not always the most patient bunch.

Offering company shares and dividends

Rather than offering potential investors digital assets, you could opt to grant them a share of your company or project in exchange for their money. When taking this approach, you can ask for as much or as little per share as you personally like, but you have to ensure these shares represent some value.

You can give your company shares value by paying weekly, monthly, or even quarterly dividends to shareholders. Once again, by doing so you incentivize potential investors to spread the word about your company or project, which is essentially an invaluable form of free marketing for whatever you are trying to achieve.

To make the offer even sweeter for potential investors, you can choose to pay out dividends in bitcoin. Even though these amounts will be very small in the early days, investors will start to see some form of return of their initial investment. Plus, it will give everyone a public hint of how the company/project is faring and what can be improved in the near future.

The same principle of paying dividends in bitcoin can be applied to potential investors who want to stick to traditional payment methods, rather than buy bitcoin first. Once they have sent you the designated funds, you can still pay their dividends in bitcoin, in order to get them acquainted with the monetary aspect of this digital currency, assuming they are willing to agree to those terms.

Holding Bitcoins for the Future

Bitcoin attracts a lot of speculators from all over the world. Considering that the bitcoin price fluctuates constantly, you could gain a lot of money by buying bitcoin at a relatively low price in the hopes of earning a profit in the future.

Keeping in mind there will only be 21 million bitcoins in existence by 2140, it only seems logical that the price per bitcoin will increase over time. Whether or not that will actually be the case remains to be seen.

Driving your investment vehicle forwards

Bitcoin is often referred to as an *investment vehicle,* even though that term is thrown around quite loosely by many people. In the early days of bitcoin, people would buy up cheap coins in the hopes of not only growing the network by giving out free BTC, but also because the price per coin would hopefully increase. And that certainly fits the description of an investment vehicle.

That said, the bitcoin price has come a long way since the digital currency's inception in 2009. In the early days, every bitcoin being mined was virtually worthless, a trend that continued for quite some time until the network started to grow and more people shared an interest in bitcoin.

As interest in bitcoin grew, the market price experienced a slow but steady uptrend between 2010 and 2013. 2013 was an especially interesting year for bitcoin, when the price per coin rapidly increased and reached an all-time high of U.S. $1,163. As was to be expected, this price could not hold its ground, and the value started dropping again slowly after.

10,000 bitcoins for two pizzas?

The whole "value of bitcoin" debate started picking up mainstream media attention when a user named Laszlo on BitcoinTalk (www.bitcointalk.org), an online forum where like-minded souls can discuss bitcoin, offered a bounty of 10,000 BTC for two pizzas. Another BitcoinTalk forum user offered to order two pizzas from Dominos and have them delivered to Laszlo's house in exchange for the bounty.

On that day, the very first "official" bitcoin transaction for a product and service was recorded on the blockchain. May 22, 2010, and now the date 22 May going forward is known as Laszlo's Pizza Day around the world, celebrated with events in various countries. And in fact, some bitcoin enthusiasts do meet up on May 22 to enjoy a slice of pizza together while discussing everything related to bitcoin and the blockchain.

After that day, more and more people started to see the potential value of bitcoin, and investors scooped up as many coins as they could. Wealthy individuals, such as the Winklevoss twins (of Facebook-founding fame), set a goal of having 1 percent of all bitcoins in circulation in their possession at all times. Quite an ambitious goal, especially when you take into consideration there will be a total of 21,000,000 coins by 2140.

Until the end of 2014 and early 2015, the bitcoin price kept falling lower and lower, despite an increase in merchant adoption and the number of wallets created. Some financial experts saw this as the downfall of bitcoin, whereas others saw it as merely the beginning of a new era for the disruptive digital currency and perhaps of some currency speculators being shaken out of the market. In simple financial terms, there was a bubble in the bitcoin price followed by a crash which has seen the price return to levels comparable prior to the bubble. At the time of this writing, it remains unclear who was right. But one thing's for sure: Reports about bitcoin's demise are greatly exaggerated. Figure 4-1 shows the ups and downs of bitcoin's price through the years.

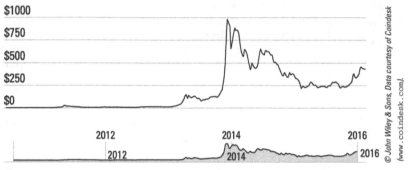

Figure 4-1: The price of bitcoin has fluctuated.

Hoarding your booty

So many people own various amounts of bitcoin as an investment that a new problem has been created: Investors who bought bitcoin at a low — or very high — price are holding on to their bitcoin balance in the hopes of recouping their investment or making a profit.

With so many coins being kept out of active circulation for an unknown period of time, this raises concern regarding the future of bitcoin. As the price keeps drifting horizontally on the charts, rather than vertically, the sudden demand seems to have slowed down. On the other hand, with multiple people holding a vast amount of coins, bitcoin could be only one sell order away from plummeting to pre-2013 values.

As is the case with any form of major investment, there's always a chance that someone liquidates their assets because they're getting impatient. And bitcoin is no different in that regard. Strangely enough, hoarding also creates a positive side effect.

Bitcoin is one of those digital currencies that has a fixed supply of coins to be released. By the time you're reading this book, we will be at 75 percent of the total amount being in circulation. Even so, there is still quite a scarcity, as not all of these coins are being spent or sold to other investors.

That leaves interested parties with a smaller amount of coins to purchase, which should in turn, eventually, push the price up again. Depending on how much some of the original coin hoarders paid for their stash of bitcoin, it may take a long while until the BTC price settles at a point where they consider selling off some assets.

Regardless of how you look at the situation, hoarding is a problem in the bitcoin world. But keep in mind this digital currency is only six years old, and there is still a lot of time left to grow and gain more adoption on a global level. How that will affect the hoarding problem, as well as the views on bitcoin as an investment vehicle, remains to be seen.

Check out the bitcoin price chart at the following website for up-to-the-minute info on what your BTC is worth. We recommend setting the view to 1W (one week) for the most comprehensive picture over time: `https://bitcoinwisdom.com/markets/bitstamp/btcusd`.

Earning Bitcoin

Rather than buying bitcoin from an exchange (as discussed in Chapter 2), there are other ways to obtain bitcoin. There are several ways to "earn" bitcoin while you actively contribute to the community and learn about new aspects that may be of interest to you in the future.

The first thing to do is sign up to a bitcoin forum, and then read on. Here are two good examples:

- ✔ BitcoinTalk (`http://bitcointalk.org`)
- ✔ Bitcoin subReddit (`www.reddit.com/r/Bitcoin/`)

Earning through forums

Most online bitcoin discussions take place on the BitcoinTalk forums (at `www.bitcointalk.org`). And as this forum has grown in popularity over the years, opportunities to make money have arisen as well. Especially for new and established bitcoin companies, the BitcoinTalk forum is an interesting place to advertise their business.

Forum signatures (placed at the bottom of forum profiles and visible on every post a user makes) allow BitcoinTalk users to earn a small amount of bitcoins every time they make a constructive post or topic on the forum. The person organizing this forum signature campaign keeps track of the number of posts you make during a week and pays the according amount at an agreed upon time. Engaging in discussions with a well-constructed opinion or answer is one way to do that. Or if you have a question you would like to see answered, the creation of a topic also counts as one post. Additionally, you may be rewarded for every constructive reply on your own topic.

Rewards for forum signature campaigns depend on various factors. First of all, the company looking for people to advertise its service may have a small or large budget, and the payout per valid post correlates to that amount. In some cases, that amount can be next to nothing, whereas in other cases, it might be quite substantial. This all depends on which product or service the company is looking to promote, and how much user interaction it receives based on the forum signature campaign in general.

Secondly, some forum signature campaigns limit the number of posts you can make during a payout period. A *payout* period is an agreed-upon amount of time during which the user can make posts to promote the signature campaign. Most signature campaigns pay out users on a weekly basis, and the company running the advertisement can decide to only allow a maximum number of posts per week. Any post over that amount is not rewarded.

One of the most important factors to determine whether or not a forum signature is right for you depends on your own user rank on BitcoinTalk. Members who are active and often participate in conversations will see their forum rank increase. The higher your forum user rank, the higher your forum signature payout per post will be.

Legendary users (users with a level of "forum activity" of over 850) and *Hero* users (users with a level over 500) usually earn the most of any user class and are hardly ever limited to a maximum amount of posts per payout period.

Spamming the forum with clutter and short messages can lead to being banned and disqualified from the forum signature campaign.

More information on BitcoinTalk signature campaigns can be found at: `https://bitcointalk.org/index.php?board=52.0`.

Earning through jobs

Several platforms exist where you can find a job that pays in bitcoin. Whether you want to make a *career* out of working for bitcoin is a different matter entirely, but completing micro tasks is a great way to build a reputation and earn some money on the side.

Unfortunately, hardly any of these tasks pays a substantial amount, though some opportunities can lead to other doors being opened in the future. And those doors can lead to interesting job opportunities, even though those are more the exception than the rule.

One thing to keep in mind when completing any sort of task in exchange for bitcoin is that you have to deal with legitimate people and companies only. If a specific task needs to be completed for a certain company, your chances of getting paid are much higher compared to dealing with random individuals.

Additionally, there is no such thing as getting paid up front in the bitcoin world. Similar to how regular jobs work, you have to provide the service or goods first before you get paid. There are usually no written contracts between both parties to warrant a payment, so tread carefully when jumping at an opportunity.

Other than small tasks, there are always job opportunities from major bitcoin companies or from companies willing to explore the world of digital currency. If you have coding knowledge — preferably in languages like PHP, SQL, JavaScript, or C# — there should be ample job opportunities to choose from.

Bitcoin is still a brand new industry, and many companies think they have what it takes to deliver the "next big thing." As a result, people who find their job in the bitcoin world right now — and surely in the years to come — will not only receive their wage in BTC, but company shares (or stock) as well. Working from home is a possibility, though most jobs require a physical presence wherever the company is located.

Depending on your location, any form of bitcoin income might be subject to taxation. This situation is different for every individual country. We advise you to check with your local government or tax revenue office to see whether bitcoin is taxable in your country.

Earning through faucets

One of the easiest ways of earning parts of a bitcoin comes in the form of so-called faucets. A *faucet* is a website that lets users claim a tiny amount of bitcoin in a certain time period, which can range anywhere from minutes to days.

Don't expect to get rich overnight by visiting various bitcoin faucets, because most of them will pay next to nothing. Then again, you're doing nothing to earn it.

Bitcoin faucets operate on a simple principle: They keep on giving out tiny chunks of bitcoin as long as there are advertisers willing to spend money to have their banner hosted on the faucet website (clicking the advertising banners generates small revenue for the hosting website). Fractional amounts of bitcoin are regularly distributed, and the funds have to come from somewhere. In most cases, bitcoin faucet operators pay out of their own pocket for the first weeks or months until they can attract enough traffic and secure some advertising deals for their website.

For the novice user, bitcoin faucets are a great way to collect fractional amounts of bitcoin. However, visiting bitcoin faucets all day long would still only get you $2 or $3 maximum, so there is trade-off in terms of whether it is worth your time. In most cases, it isn't worth your time, because there are more productive ways to earn bitcoin, such as forum signature campaigns or completing micro tasks (see the previous sections for more on these).

You can find more information on bitcoin faucets at `https://en.bitcoin.it/wiki/Bitcoin_faucet`.

Part II
Banking with Bitcoin

Four Types of Bitcoin Wallets

- ✔ Software wallet: An application that lives on your computer and keeps track of your bitcoins
- ✔ Hardware wallet: A physical, portable device where you can store your bitcoins
- ✔ Paper wallet: Not really paper, this stores your bitcoins in a very secure way that's not connected to the blockchain, also known as cold storage
- ✔ Web wallet: A third-party company that acts as a middleman, holding your bitcoins and administering your account

Check out a free Web article on the blockchain at `www.dummies.com/extras/bitcoin`.

In this part . . .

✔ Keep your bitcoins in different kinds of wallets.

✔ Know all about bitcoin transactions, network confirmations, and fees.

✔ Peek under the hood to discover blockchain technology and what it can do for you.

Chapter 5

Your Bitcoin Wallet

. . . .

In This Chapter

▶ Understanding how wallets work

▶ Reviewing the various types of wallets

▶ Keeping your wallet secure

. . . .

*I*f you've read any of the other chapters so far, you'll have spotted plenty of references to a *bitcoin wallet*. So, no doubt you're asking yourself, "What *is* a bitcoin wallet?" This chapter reveals all!

As the name suggests, a bitcoin wallet is the place where you store all the relevant information for your bitcoins. Not only does a bitcoin wallet serve as a way to store your funds — similar to a bank account — it also allows you to send and receive funds.

It's no exaggeration to say that a bitcoin wallet is the single most important thing to protect for as long as you are involved in bitcoin and digital currency.

As soon as you have the bitcoin wallet software installed on your computer or mobile device (as discussed in Chapter 2), you will be presented with a bitcoin wallet address. That bitcoin wallet address is the identification number by which you are known as a member of the bitcoin network. It acts as your account number to send, receive, and store bitcoins.

Unlocking Public and Private Keys

There is more to a bitcoin wallet than just the address itself. It also contains the public and private key for each of your bitcoin addresses. Your bitcoin *private key* is a randomly generated string (numbers and letters), allowing bitcoins to be spent. A *private* key is always mathematically related to the bitcoin wallet address, but is impossible to reverse engineer thanks to a strong encryption code base.

If you don't back up your private key and you lose it, you can no longer access your bitcoin wallet to spend funds.

You can read more about private keys at `https://en.bitcoin.it/wiki/Private_key`.

As mentioned, there is also a *public key*. This causes some confusion, as some people assume that a bitcoin wallet address and the public key are the same. That is not the case, but they are mathematically related. A bitcoin wallet address is a hashed version of your public key.

Every public key is 256 bits long — sorry, this is mathematical stuff — and the final *hash* (your wallet address) is 160 bits long. The public key is used to ensure you are the owner of an address that can receive funds. The public key is also mathematically derived from your private key, but using reverse mathematics to derive the private key would take the world's most powerful supercomputer many trillion years to crack.

Besides these key pairs and a bitcoin wallet address, your bitcoin wallet also stores a separate log of all of your incoming and outgoing transactions. Every transaction linked to your address will be stored by the bitcoin wallet to give users an overview of their spending and receiving habits.

Last but not least, a bitcoin wallet also stores your user preferences. However, these preferences depend on which wallet type you're using and on which platform. The Bitcoin Core client, for example, has very few preferences to tinker around with, making it less confusing for novice users to get the hang of it.

Your bitcoin wallet generates a "master" file where all of the preceding details are saved. For computer users, that file is called wallet.dat. It's saved on a Windows machine, for example, in the C:\User\Yourname\Documents\AppData\Roaming\Bitcoin\folder. Make sure to create one or multiple backups of this wallet.dat file on other storage devices, such as a USB stick or memory card. The bitcoin wallet software will let you import a wallet.dat file in case your previous file is damaged or lost, restoring your previous settings, including any funds associated with your bitcoin wallet address.

More information on importing private keys and wallet.dat files can be found at `https://en.bitcoin.it/wiki/How_to_import_private_keys`. Also check out the nearby sidebar "Inside your private key."

Inside your private key

The private key to your bitcoin wallet is the most important piece of information that has to be kept safe and secure at all times. This "secret number" allows bitcoins in your wallet to be spent, as it is used to verify you are the legitimate "owner" of the coin balance associated with your wallet address.

A bitcoin wallet, regardless of whether it is installed on a computer or mobile device, can contain more than one private key, all of which are saved in the wallet. dat file.

Private keys for bitcoin wallets are usually 256-bit numbers, which can be represented in multiple ways. The following is a bitcoin private key in its hexadecimal format. A 256-bit key in hexadecimal is 32 bytes or 64 characters long, with each character ranging from 0–9 or A–F:

E9 87 3D 79 C6 D8 7D C0 FB 6A 57 78 63 33 89 F4 45 32 13 30 3D A6 1F 20 BD 67 FC 23 3A A3 32 62

Without knowing the corresponding private key, funds stored in a specific bitcoin wallet address can't be spent. Reverse engineering the private key from the public key and/or the wallet address itself is virtually impossible. This makes bitcoin one of the toughest encryption protocols to crack.

However, seeing the value of a public key (which also is the bitcoin address) does not require you to know the private key at all. The public key associated with a wallet address is enough to receive bitcoins, and also to view the balance itself. But without the private key, there is no way to spend the balance associated with your bitcoin wallet address.

Should your private key ever be compromised, the only way to protect your bitcoin balance is by spending it to a different output that is secure (a different wallet address for example). Bitcoins can only be spent once, and are non-reversible, and once the full balance of an address has been spent, the private key becomes useless.

Getting Your Hands on a Bitcoin Wallet

When you take paper money out of a bank machine, you need to put it somewhere — usually your wallet or your purse. Surprise, surprise: Bitcoins also need to be stored somewhere, too, allowing you to access them when you want. Several variations of bitcoin wallets are available, such as software wallets, hardware wallets, paper wallets, and web wallets. You can think of your bitcoin wallet just like your physical purse or wallet, although you can't keep a photo of your kids in it.

All bitcoins are stored in a large database or public ledger called the *blockchain*. Bitcoin uses software that interacts with the blockchain, allowing you to visibly see your balance at any given time. You can find out more about the blockchain in Chapter 7, but it's important to know about when looking at wallets because the blockchain is the backbone of bitcoin, and bitcoin couldn't work without it: Each bitcoin wallet reads the blockchain to confirm your bitcoin balance.

A bitcoin wallet can also hold many bitcoin addresses and ties them all together for you.

Software wallets

A *software wallet* is a bitcoin application that sits on your computer's hard drive and allows you complete control and great security, because each bitcoin you hold is only accessible on your own computer. This software, called Bitcoin Core, is developed and supported by the Bitcoin Foundation.

When your software wallet is installed, it creates the wallet.dat file that holds the data that relates to your personal bitcoin wallet.

To find out how to get a software wallet, visit `http://Bitcoin.org` and click the Get started with Bitcoin link.

The bitcoin software wallet is *open source* (meaning that the source code for the software is fully accessible by anyone who wishes to see the code). Open source ensures transparency and allows users to check the source code to ensure it contains no malware or other suspicious code that could damage your computer or jeopardize your security. It also means, if you're a bit of a technical whiz kid, you can compile applications such as Bitcoin Core wallet yourself (although we're not the computer experts to ask about this).

Syncing your wallet

To ensure that your software wallet is giving you the most up-to-date information about your account, you should *sync* (technical speak for a refresh and update) it on a regular basis. Different computers and tablets perform this sync in their own way, so be sure to check out how to sync a program on your device.

When you first download and install the Bitcoin Core software client — which you'll need to download to use a software wallet — the installation may take a few days because it needs to download the history of every transaction ever created from 2009 to the very latest transaction.

Every time you close the wallet either with a computer shutdown or by closing the application, remember to sync again next time you open the application.

Securing your wallet

The Bitcoin Core client allows you to encrypt a password — which we recommend you do, because with encryption, if somebody got their hands on your hard drive, they would need to know the password to get access to your bitcoins. And if you've set a hard-to-guess password, you can rest assured that your bitcoins are as safe as can be.

Every time you send bitcoins from the wallet, you're asked for the password you used to secure the wallet, so make sure you set a memorable one.

Backing up your wallet

When you create your bitcoin wallet, please ensure to back it up within the software. You can put the backup file onto a USB flash drive or external hard drive, and with it being encrypted, it means you will be safe in the knowledge you can have access to your bitcoins again if something bad were to happen to your computer.

Multiple bitcoin addresses

When you install the bitcoin wallet, it allows you to create multiple addresses as required, which means you can have an address dedicated to people who send you bitcoins.

Hardware wallets

Some companies are now developing hardware versions of a bitcoin wallet that allow you to store your bitcoins onto a physical, portable device. If you have this device with you, all you need to do to spend your bitcoins is connect it to the Internet and begin your shopping spree (or the rather more sober transferral of bitcoin).

Paper wallets

Owning a *paper wallet* means the address that holds the bitcoins has not yet been connected to the live blockchain, and so is not "active." Until the wallet is connected to the blockchain, it is considered to be in *cold storage* (bitcoin jargon for an account being offline).

You can always check the balance of any bitcoin address by searching the blockchain, but to spend it you would need to associate the bitcoin address of the paper wallet to a wallet that is online.

Paper wallets are classed as the most secure method of holding your bitcoins if you do not intend to spend them initially.

When you send bitcoins to an address, they are stored in the blockchain, but to be able to spend them, you will need the *private key*. As mentioned, this is a long alphanumeric string of characters, and when linked to a bitcoin wallet, any coins associated will be accessible to spend via that wallet. So, a paper wallet is a very secure way of holding your bitcoins, but as with anything involving banking, you need to ensure you look after your private key.

When you create a paper wallet, make sure you are not connected to the Internet: If you are connected, there's a chance that malware could intercept your data, record your private key, and have access to any coins held in your bitcoin address at a later date.

Check out the following section on creating a paper wallet for a step-by-step guide to setting one up.

Here's a quick tutorial on how you can create a paper wallet. The service we used for this process is BitAddress.org, the easiest place to create new paper wallets for bitcoins. In the following figures, you will see the steps you need to take in order to have your own paper wallet ready for usage within minutes.

1. Visit `http://bitaddress.org` in your favorite browser.

2. You will see a screen similar to Figure 5-1 that automatically generates new bitcoin addresses and private keys for you. Move the mouse pointer around a bit and enter random text in the text box to increase the randomness of your addresses and keys.

3. Don't save the private key and QR codes presented to you. Instead, click Paper Wallet.

4. Select the number of addresses you want to generate.

5. Hide the art if you prefer to, even though the standard design looks great. Glick the Generate button to start the generation process for your number of paper wallets.

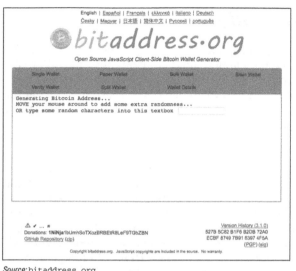

Source: bitaddress.org

Figure 5-1: Generating new bitcoin addresses.

6. To save the paper wallets or simply print them out, click the Print button.

7. Print your paper wallets or save them as a PDF to your hard drive. Saving them as a file is not recommended though, as it is best to print out these wallets as soon as they are generated.

8. Scan the QR code on the *left* side with your mobile bitcoin client, or enter the public key address in the bitcoin client on your computer. In doing so, you can start transferring bitcoins onto your paper wallet. The private key, used to verify ownership of the account in order to spend the balance, can be scanned with the QR code on the *right* side.

Crypto wallet cards

Prypto offers a product called the Crypto wallet that has two cards: One is your bitcoin address, and the other is your private key, covered up by a scratch-off film (so, until it is removed, nobody knows what it is). This adds an extra security step to help you keep your bitcoins safe and sound. For more information, check out `http://cryptowalletcards.com`.

Web wallets

Some companies offer bitcoin wallet services. They effectively act as a middleman to hold your bitcoins and allow you to spend and deposit as you want, taking responsibility for the administration and security of your account. It also means that the company will ask you for personal information, thus making this a non-anonymous environment.

If you intend to use a third-party bitcoin wallet, ensure you can trust the company behind the service. In the past, there have been several companies that held bitcoins for people, but have rapidly disappeared, been hacked, or gone bust. For example, in February 2014, the major bitcoin exchange Mt. Gox ceased operating and closed suddenly, with lots of people losing their bitcoins that had been stored with them. So choose with care. In general, exchanges or other third-party companies that hold funds on your behalf should be treated with caution. The country where that company is registered will have its own requirements as to how well regulated that company must be. Because regulations of bitcoin as a financial service or product are still being developed in many areas of the world, you should choose a country with a strong background in regulating financial services, such as the United States, United Kingdom, or the Isle of Man. While regulations are developed, we urge extreme care when storing funds on a third-party exchange or similar company — and don't store any more than you need or more than you can afford to lose should the worst come to pass.

Various types of third-party solutions are available as web wallets. Here are some examples:

✔ **Bitcoin exchanges:** Some like to hold their coins or a portion of their coins on exchanges to allow them to take advantage of being easily accessible to trade their coins for either fiat currencies like USD, GBP, or EUR, or for alternative crypto-currencies. Although this may be convenient, we do *not* recommend it for the reasons mentioned earlier.

✔ **Dedicated wallet service:** There are dedicated bitcoin wallet service websites with no exchange connection.

✔ **Mobile wallets:** As with all the majority of software released today, companies are offering web solutions for multiple mobile devices.

Setting up a Bitcoin Address

Similar to the way e-mail addresses work, a bitcoin address can be used to both send and receive data — or in this case, bitcoins. That said, there is one major distinction to be made between bitcoin addresses and e-mail addresses. People can have multiple bitcoin addresses they can use to send and receive transactions. In fact, it is advisable to use a brand new bitcoin address for every transaction, which may or may not be manageable for individual users depending on how many transactions they intend to process on a daily basis. Contrary to popular belief, the generation of a new bitcoin address does not require an active Internet connection.

 A bitcoin address is an identifier representing a possible destination — or origin — for a bitcoin transaction. Every bitcoin address is between 26 and 35 alphanumeric characters in length and can start with a 1 or a 3. Creating new or additional bitcoin addresses can be done free of charge through the installed bitcoin software, or you can obtain a bitcoin wallet address from an exchange or online wallet provider.

 One important aspect of a bitcoin address to keep in mind is that every address is case sensitive and exact. A bitcoin address like the following has both uppercase and lowercase letters in its string of characters:

1L5wSMgerhHg8GZGcsNmAx5EXMRXSKR3He

Changing an uppercase letter to a lowercase letter or vice versa would result in an invalid recipient address, and the funds would not be transferred.

 There *is* always an off chance of an invalid address being accepted as a recipient, but that only occurs once every 4.29 billion transactions.

 We advise using a different bitcoin address for every transaction. Keep in mind that there is — technically — nothing wrong with using the same address over and over again, but using a new address for every transaction creates an additional layer of privacy protection.

 Every bitcoin address is a specific invoice for a payment. Once a payment has been received to your bitcoin address, there is no reason for the sender to retain that data. However, in the event of a wallet address being lost or compromised, any future payments to this same address would be sent to a "black hole," and be forever lost to the original address owner. This is the main reason why it is advised to use a brand new bitcoin address for every transaction — in order to avoid potential loss.

More information on reusing addresses can be found at `https://en.bitcoin.it/wiki/Address_reuse`.

Grasping Your Wallet Securely

In the same way that you wouldn't walk around with your real wallet hanging out of your back pocket, or keep your bank card PIN number on a piece of paper inside that wallet, you need to be security conscious about your bitcoin wallet, too. This section gives you tips and advice on keeping your virtual wallet safe.

Securing mobile wallets

A mobile bitcoin wallet is convenient to use, because it can be installed on either a tablet or smartphone. Either of these devices is more often than not in close proximity to everyday consumers and doesn't require users to take additional items with them wherever they go.

Similar to how a desktop bitcoin wallet works, having access to an Internet connection — either through mobile data or WiFi — is a great plus when it comes to sending and receiving transactions. However, this is not a must, as most bitcoin wallets allow users to send and receive funds through NFC or Bluetooth Low Energy connection. In return, this makes mobile wallets more versatile compared to their computer counterparts, which is also part of the reason why bitcoin has received a lot of appreciation from its users.

In terms of security, the story with mobile bitcoin wallets is not all that different from a piece of software installed on your computer. The private key — which allows you to spend bitcoins from your wallet — is stored on your mobile device itself. As a security measure, this reduces the risk of the private key falling into the wrong hands.

However, there is a potential risk in doing so as well. Given the current rate at which technology — and consumer behavior — evolves, smartphones and tablets are being replaced at a rapid pace. Considering that your private key is stored on that mobile device, it is important to make a backup as soon as you install the mobile bitcoin wallet of your choice.

Depending on which type of mobile wallet you're using, a backup feature is included in the software itself. A copy of your backup can then be exported to cloud services such as Dropbox or Google Drive, or even sent to yourself via e-mail. Any application you have installed on your mobile device with backup capabilities should be available to use.

Authentication is an important security measure to prevent funds being stolen or misused by someone who "borrows" your phone. Most mobile wallets enable a PIN code system, forcing users to enter a four- to six-digit code before accessing the wallet itself. Failure to provide the correct PIN code within a certain amount of attempts will automatically lock down the wallet. The bitcoin wallet owner will be notified either via SMS or e-mail with instructions on how to unlock the mobile wallet again.

All in all, mobile bitcoin wallets can provide the best solutions when balancing the needs of security and convenience, but it all depends on the individual user in the end. If users are careless with their device, or forget to back up their private key, there is no option to restore access to their mobile bitcoin wallet. Bitcoin allows users to take full control — and full responsibility — at every step, which includes responsibilities such as backing up their mobile wallet.

Securing online wallets — or not

You could easily draw a parallel between online bitcoin wallet providers and financial institutions such as banks. Both services handle your personal funds, and you can check the balance, as well as send and receive funds at any time. But you are trusting a bank to keep your funds safe, and that's not what bitcoin is about. Ever since bitcoin's inception, trust has played an integral role in the development of this ideology. We believe Satoshi Nakamoto envisioned that the future development of bitcoin would eventually lead to a "trustless" society, where all interactions were done between people directly, without using any third-party service.

An online bitcoin wallet service is very convenient, but it's also a tremendous security risk. Being able to store bitcoins online and accessing them from the browser at any time sounds like an advantage, but in doing so, the user is relying on the online wallet provider to be honest at all times.

Online wallet providers are third-party services, as they will control your funds for you. Additionally, the biggest security risk is that, even though you know your online wallet address, you don't have access to your private key. In the event of the online wallet service shutting down or being hacked, you would have no control over the funds being stored in your wallet.

On top of that, you are responsible for protecting your personal mobile wallet service account. Most online bitcoin wallet platforms provide options such as two-factor authentication (as discussed in Chapter 2). And although that additional layer of security protects the user from harm — in *most* cases, as no system is truly perfect — it will not prevent your funds from being stolen if the online wallet service itself is hacked.

If you already have the mindset of wanting to control your own funds at any given time, there's no reason why you should even consider using an online bitcoin wallet. As convenient as these services may be, there are risks to your funds, because you are not in control of your funds at any given time. Online bitcoin wallets are not what Satoshi Nakamoto envisioned when he created bitcoin.

Securing paper wallets

A bitcoin paper wallet can be best described as a document containing all the data necessary to generate private keys, effectively forming a "wallet of private keys." But that is not its only purpose, because a paper wallet can also be used to store bitcoins safely and securely, in which case the paper itself also includes public keys and redeemable codes.

The main purpose of a redeemable code is to use it as a means of funding and "redeeming" funds associated with a certain bitcoin wallet address. However, it is important to note that paper wallets should only be used once, because a paper wallet is not a bitcoin wallet intended for daily use.

Paper wallets can serve many purposes. A bitcoin paper wallet makes for a great gift when introducing friends, family, and loved ones to bitcoin. Or you can give someone a paper wallet as a tip, to show your appreciation for something the other person has done. Redeeming a paper wallet as a gift or tip requires recipients to have a bitcoin wallet installed on their computer or mobile device, through which they can import the private key associated with that address.

Regardless of how you look at it, paper wallets are a very secure way of storing bitcoin. A paper wallet is not connected to the Internet, can't be hacked, and is not a third party you rely on. However, it is a *paper* wallet, making it subject to theft, fire or water damage, getting lost, or being redeemed by someone else. Storing a paper wallet inside a vault or safe deposit box is a good way of securing your funds, but it's not too practical for most users.

Chapter 6

Bitcoin Transactions

. . . .

. . . .

*T*he concept of a bitcoin transaction is quite simple to explain — how's that for a good bit of news to start a chapter with?

First and foremost, a *bitcoin transaction* is a transfer of digital ownership of a certain amount of BTC on the bitcoin network. For example, if you own 5 bitcoin, and you send 2 bitcoin to user "Joe," you are effectively transferring the digital ownership of those 2 BTC to Joe's wallet. The other 3 BTC remain in your wallet, as you are still the digital owner of that amount.

This chapter talks you through the basics of transactions and answers some of the common questions I've been asked about the exchange of BTC.

Figuring Out How Transactions Work

At its simplest, a transaction works by you giving someone else a designated amount of the BTC you own.

In order for a bitcoin transaction to be deemed "valid," there has to be at least one input, although multiple inputs are possible as well. An *input* is a reference to an output from a previous transaction. Note that every input associated with a bitcoin transaction has to be an unspent output of a previous transaction. Furthermore, every input in a bitcoin transaction must be digitally signed, which occurs through the private key associated with the bitcoin address initiating the transfer of BTC.

If multiple inputs are associated with one bitcoin transaction, this means that the amount being sent is coming from multiple bitcoin wallet addresses. As mentioned in Chapter 5, any bitcoin user can generate an almost infinite amount of wallet addresses, each of which can hold any amount of BTC.

Here's an example: If you send 2 BTC to lucky old "Joe" again, 1 BTC comes from wallet address #2, 0.33 BTC comes from wallet address #7, and the remainder comes from wallet address #8. In this example, wallet addresses #1, #3, #4, #5, and #6 have no actual bitcoin balance and can therefore not be used as an input because there is no unspent output associated with these addresses.

However, a bitcoin transaction can have not just multiple inputs, but multiple outputs as well. As you might expect, *multiple outputs* indicate a bitcoin transaction has been sent out to be split over multiple addresses. For example: Your 5 BTC balance will be sent to the now BTC-wealthy Joe (2 BTC) and Marie (1 BTC), and the remaining 2 BTC is sent to a different bitcoin wallet under your control. On the blockchain, this one transaction will have three different outputs, one going to Joe, one to Marie, and the third to your other bitcoin wallet address.

Sending a bitcoin payment can be denominated in a multitude of *satoshi*, the smallest increment of bitcoin transactions (8 decimal points after the period). Because bitcoin is so divisible compared to traditional fiat currency, the value of 1 satoshi can vary greatly. Whereas 1 satoshi is worth next to nothing today, it could be worth a handful of cents — or even dollars — in the future, as bitcoin adoption becomes a mainstream trend. (However, all of this is based on pure speculation, covered in Chapter 4.)

Bitcoin and cash payments are not so different in terms of transactions. The amount of bitcoin associated with all of the transaction inputs combined can be greater than the amount of money being spent, which creates "change." With traditional fiat currency, change is issued to the customer in either bills or coins. With bitcoin, change is issued in the form of digital ownership of BTC associated with your wallet address. Should the amount of inputs be greater than the amount associated with the transaction outputs, an additional output to the originating address will be created for the "change" amount.

There are several ways to send a bitcoin transaction to another bitcoin user. First of all, you can ask the recipient's bitcoin address and send the money through the bitcoin software on your computer or mobile device. For mobile users, there is an easier alternative in the form of scanning a QR code, generated by the recipient. Every type of bitcoin software allows users to create QR codes, which can include the wallet address to send funds to, as well as the total amount to be paid.

What if I receive a bitcoin when my computer is powered off?

Bitcoin is often referred to as *Internet money*, not only because it is most commonly used on the Internet, but also because you need an active Internet connection in order to use the software properly. But there is no reason to be connected to the Internet on a 24/7 basis, not even to receive transactions.

Once your bitcoin wallet address has been generated, it remains active on the blockchain for pretty much an eternity — or at least for as long as the blockchain exists in its current uncompromised state. Whether you have a synchronized bitcoin software client — either on computer or mobile — really doesn't matter, as it will not interfere with the way you can receive bitcoin transactions to your address.

Granted, when it comes to spending bitcoin, an active Internet connection is required for regular computer and mobile users, as the transaction needs to be broadcasted to the network. In order to do that, an Internet connection is needed, whether it be through WiFi or mobile data. It doesn't even have to be a fast connection either — you just have to be online long enough to send the transaction to the bitcoin nodes on the network. This entire process usually takes less than one second to complete.

Imagine that you are receiving a bitcoin transaction, but you are not connected to the Internet at that time. The funds will still be transferred from the sender to your bitcoin wallet address, as your bitcoin address is "alive" on the blockchain at all times. However, you will not notice the funds being transferred until you connect your bitcoin software to the Internet once again, after which the transaction will show up in your wallet along with the number of network confirmations at that time.

Every bitcoin transaction is tracked by the network itself, and broadcasted through various nodes in order to check whether it is valid or not. Even if your computer or mobile device is not connected to the Internet at the time of the transaction, the transfer is registered on the blockchain. The funds of every transfer will appear in your wallet whenever you connect to the Internet again.

The principle of receiving bitcoin transactions offline can be compared to receiving e-mails while you are not near a computer. You will not know someone sent you an e-mail without an Internet connection or being near your device. Yet once you open up the e-mail client — or bitcoin client in this case — all information is synchronized with the server, or blockchain, and any new information addressed to you will start appearing after a few minutes.

An example: Your bitcoin wallet address has received a total of 5 bitcoin over the course of a certain period of time, and you are sending 2 BTC to Joe. The bitcoin transaction will have one input (the unspent outputs of the bitcoin transaction through which you received those 5 BTC) and create two different outputs when you send money to Joe. The first output will be the transaction to Joe, for the full amount of 2 BTC. The second output will be the "change" transaction, which "returns" the unspent 3 BTC to your wallet address.

More information on bitcoin QR codes can be found at `https://en.wikipedia.org/wiki/QR_code`.

Receiving Confirmations

Bitcoin confirmations are sent whenever the transaction has been validated by the miners (see Chapter 4 for more about miners — hint: No canaries or head torches are required). Every block found on the network includes a certain amount of bitcoin transactions that have taken place earlier. These transactions are then broadcasted to all bitcoin nodes in order to determine validity.

Every block that is found on the bitcoin network after a transaction has been broadcasted will — assuming the transaction is deemed valid — provide one network confirmation. As mentioned, a minimum of six network confirmations is required to "officially" deem a bitcoin transaction spendable (see the next section).

A *confirmation* in the bitcoin world means that a transaction has been deemed valid by the network. Without confirmations, a transaction is still "in between" users, and until there is any form of verification present on the blockchain, that transaction is a security risk for both parties. Granted, it can take time for transactions to confirm, but that is more of a security measure than an annoyance.

Most bitcoin wallets will show a bitcoin transaction as "spent," regardless of its amount of network confirmations. PC users may see the status as "n/unconfirmed," where n indicates the amount of network confirmations received for the transaction. Reaching a total of six confirmations can take up to an hour to achieve in most cases, although exceptions may occur.

There is no way for a bitcoin client to "force" network confirmations to appear, as this is entirely dependant on the bitcoin network itself. And with the bitcoin block time at roughly ten minutes apart, there is no way to influence the confirmation speed between blocks. That being said, there may be one deciding factor in the form of when your transaction is picked up by a network block.

Assuming your bitcoin transaction has been broadcasted to the network right before a new block is found, your first confirmation may occur rather quickly. However, should your bitcoin transaction be picked up in the next block — this entire process is random — it will take a little while longer to get that first confirmation accredited.

The general rule about transactions is as follows: A bitcoin transaction that has no confirmations on it will always be a high risk for double-spending. Briefly, a *double-spend* means that a bitcoin user can spend the amount of coins in a bitcoin wallet twice (see Chapter 10 for more on double-spending). In fact, any transaction that has less than six confirmations on it carries the same risk. However, merchant and payment processors are free to set their own number of required confirmations. This rule does not apply to bitcoin users who stick to bitcoin software on their computer though, as funds will remain "unconfirmed" until the six network confirmations have been achieved. Mobile users, depending on which wallet they choose, can spend incoming funds much faster.

Regular six confirmations

Keeping in mind that every transaction confirmation takes place whenever a new block is discovered on the bitcoin network — every ten minutes roughly — six confirmations can take up to an hour to complete. Once those six confirmations have taken place on a transaction, the coins become spendable for the recipient.

The hour it sometimes takes to complete — on average — can be seen as both a blessing and a curse. The upside of waiting for six (or more) confirmations comes in the form of transaction validity and avoiding being the victim of a double-spend attack on the bitcoin network. After all, bitcoin transactions are nonrefundable, and jumping the gun on a transaction without multiple confirmations can lead to financial disaster for the recipient.

There have been reports of six confirmations taking a few hours until a transaction is fully confirmed by the network. However, delayed confirmations are occurring less and less, as it also depends on the total hashrate on the bitcoin network being used to solve blocks.

Even though a transaction is deemed "confirmed" by the bitcoin software once it has received a total of six network confirmations, that does not make the transaction "valid" for the bitcoin protocol. When bitcoin was created, a piece of code was written in the bitcoin protocol to only consider the generation of new coins (mined blocks) valid once a total of 100 confirmations have been reached. In fact, most bitcoin mining pools (as mentioned in Chapter 4) won't credit block rewards to miners until 120 network confirmations have been received.

Double-spending

The bitcoin network itself is very secure in its own right, but there is always the risk of a *double-spend.* With a *double-spend,* as mentioned, a bitcoin user can spend the same bitcoin twice. In order to mitigate the chances of a double-spend taking place, the bitcoin network verifies each individual transaction through confirmations.

In general, the biggest potential for a double-spend attack occurs when merchants or traders act as soon as a transaction is visible on the network. These unconfirmed transactions — also known as *zero-confirmation transactions* — are a major risk in terms of double-spending. As a result of this, all bitcoin users are advised to wait for a minimum of six transaction confirmations before trying to move the funds again. The more confirmations a specific transaction has, the higher the chance of it being a legitimate transaction, and not a double-spend.

The chances of executing a bitcoin double-spend are slim to none. There is no system that is perfect in terms of security, but the bitcoin protocol is a different breed of technology that would require quite a lot of effort to pull off a double-spend. That being said, there are five potential forms of attack associated with a double-spend. These are explained in the following sections.

Race attack

Traders and merchants who accept a payment immediately on seeing "0/unconfirmed" are exposed to a double-spend, if there was a fraudulent attempt that successfully communicated one transaction to the merchant, yet communicated a different transaction that spends the same coin that was first to eventually make it into the blockchain.

Finney attack

The Finney attack is a fraudulent double-spend that requires the participation of a miner once a block has been mined. The risk of a Finney attack cannot be eliminated, regardless of the precautions taken by the merchant, but the participation of a miner is required and a specific sequence of events must occur. Therefore, this attack is not trivial, nor inexpensive, to perform and only makes sense for the attacker when the gains from the attack are significant.

Vector 76 attack

Also referred to as a *one-confirmation attack,* the vector76 is a combination of the race attack and the Finney attack such that a transaction that has even one confirmation can still be double-spent. The same protective action for the race attack (no incoming connections, explicit outgoing connection to a well-connected node) significantly reduces the risk of this occurring.

Brute force attack

The attacker submits to the merchant/network a transaction that pays the merchant, while privately mining a blockchain fork in which a double-spending transaction is included instead. After waiting for n confirmations, the merchant sends the product. If the attacker happens to find more than n blocks at this point, he releases his fork and regains his coins; otherwise, he can try to continue extending his fork with the hope of being able to catch up with the network.

>50 percent attack

Also referred to as a *51 percent attack.* If the attacker controls more than half of the network hashrate, the previous attack has a probability of 100 percent of success. Because the attacker can generate blocks faster than the rest of the network, he can simply persevere with his private fork until it becomes longer than the branch built by the honest network, from whatever disadvantage. More details may be found at `https://en.bitcoin.it/wiki/Double-spending.`

Zero confirmations

A trend has emerged in the bitcoin world where merchants do not wait around for the six full confirmations to mark a bitcoin payment as completed. Not waiting for the minimum amount of confirmations on a transaction increases the chance of becoming the victim of a double-spend attack. It is always a risk to consider a payment "completed" as long as the bitcoin network shows no confirmation on the transaction itself.

Nevertheless, merchant and payment processors have the option to determine the amount of confirmations needed to validate a bitcoin transaction. Whereas most services set that number anywhere from three to six confirmations, other services act as soon as the transaction is broadcasted to the bitcoin network in its unconfirmed state. Not only does this allow the purchase to be completed faster on the web page, it also allows for a faster order completion.

Most merchants who complete a transaction on zero confirmations sell inexpensive or digital items. For example, most bars and restaurants will consider the transaction as completed with 0 confirmations, as they are protected by the payment processor in case of a double-spend. Payment processors such as BitPay, BitKassa, and Coinbase all provide merchants some protection against double-spend attacks, even when the number of confirmations on the bitcoin transaction is set to 0.

Zero-confirmation bitcoin transactions are a great way for businesses and individuals alike to accept bitcoin payments quickly and securely, despite the risks associated with doing so. However, as long as the recipient sues a payment processor to protect against financial loss from a double-spend attack, there is no reason not to set the number of required network confirmations to zero.

Calculating Bitcoin Fees

Bitcoin is often touted as a global payment network that includes no transaction fees. Up to a certain extent, that statement is true, but it doesn't tell the entire story. No transaction fee is involved for the recipient on any bitcoin transaction coming from another user on the network. But sometimes, there is a transaction fee involved, albeit very minimal.

Transaction fees in the bitcoin world are not included in every transaction. In fact, most bitcoin wallets allow the user to optionally include a transaction fee in order to speed up the transaction itself. By speeding up, we mean a transaction including a small fee will be prioritized to be included in the next network block, whereas transactions without fees have a lower priority.

Certain exceptions to including a transaction fee don't affect the transaction speed. In the Bitcoin Core client, if your transaction is smaller than 1,000 bytes in size, has only outputs of 0.01 BTC or higher, and has a high enough priority, a transaction fee is not required. All of these conditions have to be met in order for this exception to be applicable. If these conditions are not met, a standard transaction fee of 0.0001 BTC per thousand bytes will be added. Bitcoin Core client users will notice whenever a transaction fee is included, as the client will prompt the user to either accept or reject the fee associated with the transaction. Rejecting that fee lowers the prioritization and affects the speed at which network confirmations are applied, though.

Most bitcoin transactions are around 500–600 bytes in size, and depending on the output, may or may not be subject to a 0.0001 BTC transaction fee. Including a transaction in a network block is completely random, but is affected by the transaction fee (if required). Every block leaves 50,000 bytes of room for high-priority transactions — regardless of transaction (TX) fee — to be included (roughly 100 transactions per block). After that, transactions subject to the fee of 0.00001 BTC/kilobyte are added to the block, with the highest fee-per-kilobyte transactions being included first. This process is repeated until the block size reaches a size of 750,000 bytes.

Looking at Transaction Speed

Transaction priority is determined by a rather complicated mathematical formula. Priority is calculated as follows: It is the value-weighted sum of input age (how old the transaction is) divided by the transaction size in bytes. For best measure, that weighted sum should be above 57,600,000.

As you may have guessed, sometimes there are more transactions waiting to be broadcasted than can be included in the current block. Any leftover transactions will remain in the miner's *memory pool* (a collection of transactions that have not yet been verified by the bitcoin network), and will be included in future blocks, prioritized by their transaction fee (if required).

The relaying of bitcoin transactions is also subject to whether or not a fee has been included. Relaying transactions ignores whether or not all outputs are at least 0.01 BTC or more, but only checks whether or not the transaction is labelled as "free" or not. A "free" transaction means whether or not a fee of 0.00001 BTC has been added to the transaction total. If not, the transaction is labelled as "free" and is put lower on the priority list.

More information on transaction relaying can be found at https://en.bitcoin.it/wiki/Transaction_fees#Relaying.

For more info, check out https://en.bitcoin.it/wiki/Transaction_fees#Technical_info.

Understanding Mining Fees

Bitcoin transactions are included in blocks by the bitcoin miners (see Chapter 4 for more about miners). Hence, including a transaction fee for every transaction serves as an incentive for miners to include your transaction in the next block.

Every transaction fee can be seen as a small reward to all miners who solved the block that includes your transaction(s).

The bitcoin mining process will come to a halt when all bitcoins have been mined, which is estimated to happen in 2140. It is anticipated that miners will keep solving network blocks (that include transactions) in exchange for the transaction fees included for every individual transaction. There is much debate regarding these fees and whether or not they should be increased to incentivize the miners. However, it will take many years until a consensus is reached regarding that decision, so you shouldn't worry about it right now.

Without mining fees, there is no incentive for miners to validate your transactions. Even though no one is obligated to include a transaction fee — unless decided upon otherwise by your bitcoin wallet — it is best practice to always include a minor fee in order to support the bitcoin network and the individual miners.

Dealing with Multi-Signature Transactions

You might expect that the end-user is in control of bitcoin funds at any given time. However, because the end-user is the only person with the private key belonging to their wallet address(es), a more secure solution had to be developed. Whereas leaving one user in control of one wallet for individual usage is okay, things are slightly different for companies, families, or even friends working on a project together. Trust might disintegrate quickly.

The way a regular bitcoin wallet works is as follows: One user has the private key and has full control over that bitcoin address. If two or more people create a project together, there used to be only one option available to them: Trust one of the users with the private key to the mutual wallet address. If that user wanted to cash out all the funds, the other member(s) couldn't do anything about it, because they were not in control.

Needless to say, this was a far from perfect solution, which spurred on innovation to give multiple users control of the same wallet. Eventually, a multi-signature system was developed, where multiple users control the same wallet, yet no single user has full control without the consent of at least one other person in the group. This is known as a *multi-signature account* or *multi-sig account*.

Contrary to a regular bitcoin wallet, multi-signature bitcoin addresses require multiple private keys before funds can be spent. Receiving a transaction to a multi-signature wallet works in the same way as a regular wallet, as the private key is not involved in receiving funds. When sending funds, however, every transaction is digitally signed by the bitcoin software on your device using the private key linked to your wallet address.

Multi-signature bitcoin addresses require "*m*-of-*n*" private keys in order to be able to spend funds associated with that particular bitcoin address. For example, a three-way multi-signature address will require (at least) 2-of-3 private keys belonging to that address: If three people are creating a multi-sig wallet ($m = 3$), at least two signatures are needed to send a transaction ($n = 2$).

Failure to provide two private keys to sign off on the transaction will result in the transaction not being sent out at all. Multi-signature bitcoin addresses provide more security for businesses and groups of people who share a mutual wallet address, yet for individual users, there is hardly any difference between a regular wallet and a multi-signature version. However, for those among us who take bitcoin security seriously, it would not be a bad idea to create a multi-signature wallet, even if it's just for personal use.

Armory, one of the many available bitcoin software clients, was the first wallet provider to integrate multi-signature addresses. Over a year ago, Armory unveiled its new LockBoxes feature, which is a practical representation of how to generate a multi-signature bitcoin address.

A detailed video guide can be found at https://bitcoinarmory. com/tutorials/armory-advanced-features/lockbox/ create-lockbox/.

A multi-sig example

In a group of three people — John, Dylan, and Maria — there are three possible combinations to reach 2-of-3 private keys:

✔ John and Dylan sign the transaction with their respective private keys

✔ John and Maria sign the transaction with their respective private keys

✔ Dylan and Maria sign the transaction with their respective private keys

Without this procedure being followed correctly, transactions cannot be processed.

Chapter 7

The Blockchain

In This Chapter

▶ Breaking down blocks and the blockchain

▶ Unlocking the blockchain's potential

▶ Driving the technology forward

*T*he bitcoin blockchain represents a complex feat of innovative technology. This chapter looks at a few different aspects of the bitcoin blockchain — by the time you've finished this chapter, you'll know pretty much all that you'll need to know about the blockchain and how it works with bitcoin.

But first of all, as usual, let's begin with the basics: What is the blockchain? Put simply, the *blockchain* is a public distributed ledger offering unprecedented transparency regarding the bitcoin ecosystem. It is a collection of all bitcoin transactions since its inception in 2009. Every additional transaction is logged on the bitcoin blockchain as well. Yet the technology is capable of far more than just that.

The blockchain is a technological advancement unlike anything seen before, and its decentralized nature means there is no central point of failure that can bring it down.

To watch a cool video about the blockchain, check out "Blockchain: The Information Technology of the Future" at `http:///hwww.slideshare.net/lablogga/blockchain-the-information-technology-of-the-future`.

Recording Transactions

One of the most often asked questions is why this technology is called a *blockchain*. To understand this, you first need to grasp the concept of a *block*. If the blockchain were a ledger, you could think of the original block as the first page of that ledger. Every new block thereafter on the bitcoin network contains a *hash* (a far shorter, seemingly random sequence of letters and numbers) of the previous network block. As the result, ever since the first block appeared on the network in 2009 — called the Genesis Block — there has been a chain of transactions, all of which are included in various blocks. And through those blocks, any transaction taking place today can be traced back all the way to the Genesis Block. Back to the ledger analogy, because each new page in the ledger contains a summary of the previous page or pages, it follows that the size of those ledger pages will increase. That's exactly what happens to the size of the blockchain as more data is stored within it.

Bitcoin's blockchain is most widely known for being an *open ledger,* which means it records all bitcoin transactions of the past, present, and future. Not only is the blockchain a bookkeeping tool, it also presents unprecedented transparency for the financial ecosystem. And it is that level of transparency that a lot of traditional financial institutions are afraid of. They don't like to disclose numbers and statistics, whereas the bitcoin blockchain is completely transparent in that regard. However, there is still a level of pseudonymity attached to the bitcoin blockchain, as individual users or companies are represented by a bitcoin wallet address, rather than by a name or address.

Consider the bitcoin blockchain, from a financial point of view, as a shared database of transactions. Every bitcoin *node* (a computer constantly running the bitcoin wallet software to detect and validate new bitcoin transactions) on the network owns a full copy of bitcoin's entire transaction history, from the beginning (2009) right up to now. In the future, more and more transactions will be added on top of the existing blockchain, creating a timeline of exactly how bitcoin evolved in the financial world.

Additionally, every new bitcoin block is generated in chronological order, as it contains the hash of a previous block. Otherwise, this hash would be unknown, which would lead to the block being rejected by the network. Furthermore, bitcoin network blocks of the past cannot be altered, because that would mean any block following a specific block number would have to be regenerated. That functionality is not available, nor will it ever be.

As a result of keeping a public ledger containing all of the previous bitcoin transactions between 2009 and the time you are reading this book, the blockchain continually grows in size. By the time you read this, bitcoin will have surpassed a 50GB blockchain size by quite a margin. And as more and more transactions are broadcasted on the bitcoin network, the block size will have to increase, leading to an even larger blockchain file size.

Understanding Blockchain Analysis

In 2014, a new trend started to emerge in the world of bitcoin and blockchain technology. *Blockchain analysis* is an entire new market within the bitcoin ecosystem, which has been made possible because of the blockchain's transparent nature. Whether or not blockchain analysis will be a curse or a blessing remains to be seen, as the opinions are quite divided at this time.

One thing that helps bitcoin thrive and grow as a mainstream payment method is the acquisition of insights into how people are spending bitcoins — not just in terms of which products and/or services are being bought with bitcoin, but also how long people are holding on to the coins they receive in their wallet. Just like cash, bitcoin is meant to be a payment method that can be spent anywhere at any time. Having a detailed analysis done on how long people hold on to their coins could help stimulate bitcoin adoption all around the world. And that, in a nutshell, is what blockchain analysis does.

The positive sides to blockchain analysis are not hard to find. Bitcoin is still a very young and immature financial system, and detailed analytics give industry experts valuable insights into how things can be taken to the next level:

- How are bitcoins being spent?
- Where are the most new wallets coming from?
- Is the hoarding problem being addressed, or is it growing worse?

All these questions deserve a proper answer, which is where blockchain analysis comes into the picture.

It is no secret that some of the "oldest" bitcoins recorded on the network have not been traded in years. Some people claim these coins belong to Satoshi Nakamoto, the creator of bitcoin. Others argue that these were early adopters who simply forgot about bitcoin after a while and never came back. Or maybe the private key was lost during a hard drive crash and never recovered, making the funds associated to those wallets unspendable.

Making bitcoin more user-friendly is another hurdle that can be overcome by focusing more efforts on blockchain analysis. For example, most users would find it pretty nifty to receive a text message whenever they sent or received a bitcoin transaction. Some major wallet providers already offer this functionality, but others do not. Receiving an SMS helps novice users to keep tabs on their spending habits and bitcoin balance.

Seeing Beyond "Just Transactions"

The blockchain can be used for just about anything you can imagine: tracking packages all around the world in real time, creating copyright claims, fighting online piracy, and bringing an end to counterfeit products. These are just a few of the ideas made possible by using blockchain technology. Granted, the blockchain has become well known for its financial capabilities in terms of recording transactions. But it is important to remember that blockchain technology is much more than bitcoin the currency.

Beyond the financial aspect of blockchain technology, the blockchain itself allows us to achieve much more than just a transaction ledger. Several projects are currently being developed that will allow tools such as smart contracts, digital transfer of ownership, and even copyright claims to exist on top of the blockchain. For example, here are two of them:

- ✓ **Factom:** A layer built on top of the bitcoin blockchain focusing on recordkeeping and data storage (for example, healthcare records).

- ✓ **Storj**: Rewarding users with Storj tokens for storing part of the blockchain on their computer, these tokens can then be used by the user to store some of their own data on the blockchain.

 Because of its transparent nature, the possibilities of the blockchain's technological use are nearly endless, and developers are only just discovering the tip of the iceberg in terms of the blockchain's potential. And the number of possible use cases increases every day.

Working with Blockchain Applications

In terms of blockchain application development, most of the focus is currently on financial services. That is only normal, as bitcoin is mostly focusing on bringing financial services to people in unbanked and underbanked parts of the world. Plus, the blockchain is best known for being an open ledger.

Yet there is so much unexplored potential in blockchain application development that there is no way to guesstimate what will be coming next. What we do know is that various projects are currently in development, and the non-financial ones aim to improve various aspects of everyday life. However, until these applications are put into proper coding, they are only ideas and nothing more at this point.

The idea behind blockchain applications is very similar to that of bitcoin itself: restoring power to the individual user without having to rely on centralized services or companies. Because of the blockchain's decentralized and transparent nature, blockchain applications offer unprecedented technological advantages. For more on centralization and decentralization, check out the nearby sidebar.

The blockchain's technological power comes with a steep learning curve. Developing blockchain applications is nothing to sneeze at. Even for coders, it takes a while to get acquainted with the parameters and *API call* (a tool used by developers to call on a specific operation within a platform or application) associated with bitcoin's blockchain.

The main aim of blockchain application development is improving our everyday lives by bringing transparency and accountability to existing infrastructure. Especially in terms of the financial world, both of these features are desperately needed. There is still much room left for other areas of technology to be improved by adopting the blockchain, and the years ahead will give us a better indication of what we can expect.

 Developing a proper blockchain-based application is a time-consuming process, as there is a lot of code to write and potential outcomes to take into account. On top of that, it takes quite a bit of funding to write a new blockchain application from scratch, because developers need to be paid for their efforts as well. Not that that is something to worry about in the bitcoin world — venture capitalist investment is still on the rise, despite the falling bitcoin price.

The blockchain is all about creating communities and giving individual users choices they currently do not have. It is often like-minded individuals who share an idea of how something can be done better who are drawn to each other. An obvious example would be those who create alternative crypto-currencies, also called altcoins. As a result, blockchain development is not tied to one programming language: Diversification is one of the greatest assets for blockchain developers. Whether this community spirit continues as blockchain applications become more commercial remains to be seen. There are certainly some comparisons to be drawn with the current state of blockchain development and the very early days of the Internet.

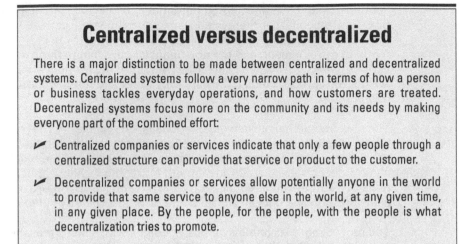

Centralized versus decentralized

There is a major distinction to be made between centralized and decentralized systems. Centralized systems follow a very narrow path in terms of how a person or business tackles everyday operations, and how customers are treated. Decentralized systems focus more on the community and its needs by making everyone part of the combined effort:

✔ Centralized companies or services indicate that only a few people through a centralized structure can provide that service or product to the customer.

✔ Decentralized companies or services allow potentially anyone in the world to provide that same service to anyone else in the world, at any given time, in any given place. By the people, for the people, with the people is what decentralization tries to promote.

Any type of blockchain application can be developed using a wide variety of programing languages, including JavaScript, Ruby, Perl, and PHP. And there are also the mobile operating systems to take into account, as blockchain applications are more than welcome on Android, iOS, Windows Phone, and Blackberry operating systems.

For more information on learning to code blockchain applications, visit https://medium.com/zapchain-magazine/the-best-resources-for-learning-to-build-bitcoin-and-block-chain-applications-8de1953506f5.

Moving Ahead to Bitcoin 2.0

Bitcoin has always been looked at as a currency for various purposes, ranging from bypassing capital controls to an investment vehicle and everything in between. Yet people are coming to the realization that bitcoin is much more than just a payment method. *Bitcoin 2.0* refers to the next generation of bitcoin applications and platforms, most of which will not be focused on the financial sector. Bitcoin 2.0 platforms and apps will use blockchain technology to have an impact on our everyday lives in other realms.

Both bitcoin and the underlying blockchain technology are capable of so much more than just serving a financial purpose, even though that is the bread and butter of this innovative protocol. Granted, there will always be a strong focus on using bitcoin and blockchain technology to further advance the financial ecosystem. There's quite a lot of room for improvements, as the financial sector has seen relatively little innovation in the past 50 years.

But there are plenty of other implementations of bitcoin and block-chain technology within our grasp as well, as shown later in this section. Using blockchains for authentication purposes, replacing traditional and insecure methods such as Facebook or Twitter authentication, is just one of the many examples of what bitcoin 2.0 can bring to the table.

The potential of bitcoin 2.0 and blockchain technology has not gone by unnoticed. Various financial institutions are looking at ways to implement the blockchain into their existing infrastructure. Even if these financial institutions don't see a viable future for bitcoin as a currency, the blockchain aspect could hold a lot of promise for the (near) future.

What makes the bitcoin 2.0 ecosystem so attractive are the blocks of data broadcasted and discovered on the network. Rather than just including transaction information, bitcoin blocks can transfer any type of data between users in a transparent manner. Digital media assets, copyright claims, and even digital insurance are just a few ideas being tossed around by various developers and engineers in the blockchain space.

Bitcoin 2.0 will also be able to improve the traditional bitcoin exchange model as we currently know it. At this time, most bitcoin exchanges allow users to store, send, and receive digital currency, without any further benefits. Bitcoin 2.0 technology can bring features such as peer-to-peer lending, interest-bearing accounts, and even the ability to lend financial securities without involvement from an intermediary such as a broker or bank.

Taking things one step further, bitcoin 2.0 applications and platforms can eliminate the need for a middleman as far as buying and selling goods is concerned. Ownership of goods can, in theory, be tied to a digital token that can be transferred to a different user on the blockchain, simultaneously with a payment for this transfer. In fact, there is a huge potential for a future portion of global e-commerce to take place on the blockchain.

And what about using bitcoin 2.0 technology to issue a virtual identity card, which can be used by owners to complete verification processes in the bitcoin world and beyond? Rather than submitting sensitive documents to a third party, who most often store them on centralized servers, a virtual identity card can be verified by the blockchain itself. The owner of the virtual identity card remains in full control of their data, while the vendor will not receive a storable copy of this information.

Using bitcoin 2.0 technology to create a new breed of decentralized marketplace is another branch of technological innovation currently in development. Trading precious metals in exchange for fiat or digital currency over the blockchain is just one example. But other aspects of life, such as digital media, can also benefit from these decentralized marketplaces. Because there is no middleman involved, overhead costs for the artists will be reduced dramatically.

Last but not least, blockchain technology is all about the community supporting this new wave of innovation. And those community members deserve voting rights in bitcoin-related projects, as well as real-life situations. Imagine that a local authority wanted to open up its spending plans to taxpayers. This could be done through an application using bitcoin 2.0 technology whereby plans, budgets, potential options, and most favored solutions could be presented, discussed, and even voted on via this technology. It has the potential to open up, democratize, and legitimate processes and decisions in a transparent fashion like nothing else can. The end result of the voting would be transparent, while no voter's personal information would be disclosed.

Creating new decentralized applications and services will be the main purpose of bitcoin 2.0 technology. This wave of innovation will empower any individual to become their own boss and create their own line of work. Whether that is being a courier for a company, or driving people around who don't like to wait for a cab, remains to be seen — Uber being an example of a decentralized service. In our view, there is very little that can't be achieved once bitcoin 2.0 goes mainstream.

Part III
Using Bitcoin in Business

Four Disadvantages of Cloud Mining

- ✔ Lack of control: You are essentially renting computing and server hardware from someone else, meaning you are not in control of those assets.

- ✔ Reliance on the honesty of someone else: If your payments seem short, there's no real way to get to the bottom of why you are not being paid as much as you think you should be.

- ✔ Maintenance and electricity fees passed along to you: Your cloud mining company has to pay to maintain the equipment, and they pass along those costs to you.

- ✔ Illegitimate or vulnerable companies: Some bitcoin cloud mining service companies may look legitimate, but they are not. Also, they may get hacked, and there is little you can do about it.

Check out a free article on bitcoin and banks at www.dummies.com/extras/bitcoin.

In this part . . .

✔ Find out about selling with bitcoin, working with bitcoin payment processors, and accepting bitcoin in your store.

✔ Read all about bitcoin and taxes, regulation, and licensing.

✔ Secure your bitcoin investment and find out about the dangers of double-spending and various types of attacks.

✔ Mining bitcoin — all about how it works and whether it's right for you.

Chapter 8

Using Bitcoin in Commerce

*U*nderstanding what bitcoin is and how it works and acquiring a little bitcoin for fun or curiosity are all well and good . . . but when it comes down to it, we're sure you want to find out a little more about using it as (virtual) cold, hard currency.

This chapter discusses the best ways to use bitcoin as a tool when selling, to substitute it for fiat currencies, and to accept and receive payments online.

Selling Your Goods for Bitcoin

When it comes to selling goods for bitcoin, you have several options to choose from. First and foremost, you can convince friends and family to embrace bitcoin and sell them goods in exchange for BTC.

But that's not what we're looking at in this chapter, as we're talking about *commerce,* not money from friends and family. This section goes over the various platforms in existence to facilitate the sale of (digital) goods in exchange for bitcoin: auction sites, using your own online store, and benefitting from online forums.

Selling on auction sites

Selling goods for bitcoin is nearly as old as the digital currency itself. However, it took a while before designated platforms started coming to life in the bitcoin world. The most obvious place to sell any product in exchange for bitcoin is an auction house or auction website, something like eBay.

Very few auction websites accept bitcoin payments at the time of writing. However, as more and more developers are exploring the option of creating decentralized auction sites and market places, that number is expected to increase over the next few years. A comprehensive list of bitcoin auction sites can be found at `https://en.bitcoin.it/wiki/Trade#Auction_sites`.

Over the years, various marketplaces *have* offered bitcoin payments as part of their service, though not all of them have been positive. Popular marketplaces such as Silk Road and Silk Road 2.0 — both of which have been notorious for illegal goods and highly questionable services — showed the bitcoin world that things needed to change if mainstream adoption is ever to be achieved.

Nearly two years ago, the first auction site started experimenting with bitcoin payments. Unlike eBay, this auction website is not just about connecting buyers and sellers from all over the world. To discourage illegal activity, auction sites come with reputation and feedback systems, something the bitcoin world desperately needed at that time.

Rather than using a centralized payment system such as PayPal, as eBay does, bitcoin auction sites use BTC as a payment method. But here is the twist: Bitcoin payments are non-reversible, forcing bitcoin auction sites to offer a different type of protection for both buyers and sellers.

Holding funds in *escrow* (meaning a third party receives the funds for a transaction and holds them until the buyer verifies the funds can be sent to the seller) is a great way to protect both the buyer and seller during a transaction. During a purchase, the buyer sends the BTC funds to an escrow address. This ensures that the seller has a chance to receive the full amount, rather than trusting the buyer to have the necessary money to pay for an item. Buyers are protected under escrow rules as well, as the escrow address holds the funds until the buyer confirms they have received the item(s) purchased from the auction site. Once everything has been verified and is deemed to be as agreed upon, the buyer notifies the escrow service to release the funds to the seller. After a transaction has been completed — successfully or not — both parties can leave feedback for each other.

Creating your own online store

Another way to use bitcoin in commerce is to set up your own online store where you offer products and/or services — physical or digital — in exchange for bitcoin.

Creating an online store and accepting bitcoin payments isn't hard to do, because the most commonly used platforms have bitcoin payment plugins ready to be used.

One easy way to get your feet wet is to create a WordPress website (check out www.wordpress.org). WordPress lends itself perfectly to various purposes, ranging from blogs to online shops and everything in between. For online commerce, plugins such as WooCommerce, WP E-Commerce, and GoUrl MarketPress let you start accepting bitcoin payments within minutes. A list of bitcoin payment plugins for Wordpress can be found at https://wordpress.org/plugins/tags/accept-bitcoin.

Besides WordPress, other popular bitcoin payments processors, including Bitpay and Coinbase (described later in this chapter) have e-commerce solutions integrated into their services, which can be linked to popular online shopping cart solutions, such as XCart and ZenCart, among others.

You'll need to decide whether you want to keep every transaction in BTC or not. There is a certain risk associated with keeping funds in bitcoin, because the bitcoin price remains quite volatile on a daily basis. Keeping funds in BTC can mean your sitting funds can either increase or decrease in value. And depending on what type of goods you're selling, and whether or not there are suppliers to pay, it might be a good idea to convert BTC funds immediately to your local fiat currency.

Selling on BitcoinTalk forums

This may be the easiest way of all: selling goods in exchange for bitcoin by posting your item for sale on the BitcoinTalk forums. To find out more about these, head over to www.bitcointalk.org. This site has a dedicated section for buying and selling items, both in physical and digital form. However, there are certain drawbacks to using the forum rather than an auction site or building your own store.

Selling an item for BTC on the BitcoinTalk forums is based on trust ratings earned by completing previous trades with other users. Assuming your account has 0 (zero) trust, at first it can be difficult to find customers willing to buy your product in exchange for a non-reversible payment method in the form of bitcoin. Solving that issue is not as hard as it may seem, though, because there are plenty of people willing to escrow the transaction (see the earlier section "Selling on auction sites" for more about escrow). The same escrow rules as the ones for bitcoin auction sites would apply: Buyer sends funds to the escrow, seller ships the item, and once the buyer verifies the delivery, funds are released to the seller.

In theory, it sounds like both parties are protected, but there is a catch. Pretty similar to how eBay works, the intermediary escrow party has to make a decision based on evidence provided whenever there is a dispute. Imagine a scenario in which you ship the item, and the buyer claims to have only received an empty box. The buyer has photographic material of the box when it arrived, unopened, and then posts a picture of the box empty without the item inside.

Unless you, as a seller, took pictures when shipping the item that everything was packaged inside the box, there is a case for a dispute. Having a tracking number associated with the shipment helps, in that delivery of the package can be tracked by the escrow. However, the final decision lies with the escrow, and as we all know, humans are fallible.

Using an auction site or building your own online store may be the best way to sell items for bitcoin. However, using the BitcoinTalk forums creates a peer-to-peer aspect to the transaction, as there are (usually) no third parties involved, except an escrow perhaps. In the end, the main goal is to satisfy the customer and receive your money in bitcoin. Pick whichever method seems best to you, and see it through till the end.

Check out the BitcoinTalk Goods section: `https://bitcointalk.org/index.php?board=51.0`.

Looking at Bitcoin Payment Solutions

As we've mentioned, in contrast to credit card transactions, which are subject to much higher fees than BTC transactions, bitcoin is a non-refundable payment method. That means that once a sender sends funds from their wallet to a recipient, that transaction can't be reversed, and funds are gone for good.

Of course the recipient could send money back to the original sender if need be. But a bitcoin payment cannot be cancelled or charged back, unlike credit card transactions. The reason is simple: Credit cards are issued by a central financial institution, which can be called upon to request a refund. With bitcoin, there is no central authority backing the digital currency, and users are solely responsible for storing and sending BTC funds.

There is no reason why bitcoin transactions should ever be made subject to chargebacks either. Every bitcoin transaction is broadcasted on the blockchain, a public ledger collecting all BTC transfers from the past, present, and future (see Chapter 7 for more on the blockchain). The blockchain makes it clear for everyone in the world to see where funds from "address A" are being sent to and for what amount.

Which brings us to another aspect of bitcoin and chargebacks that is important to keep in mind. Whenever a customer sells bitcoin to a customer, whether directly or through an exchange, it is key never to use a reversible payment method. For example, if you're selling BTC to Jonas, and he wants to pay for it in PayPal, the deal should never go through. The reason for that is simple: Traditional payment methods such as PayPal (www.paypal.com), Skrill (www.skrill.com), and credit card transactions are subject to fraud and chargebacks.

PayPal is an especially annoying platform to use when selling bitcoin, for multiple reasons. First of all, PayPal doesn't offer seller protection when dealing with "digital goods." Secondly, at the time of writing, bitcoin is still viewed as a "digital good" by PayPal's Terms of Service. Should the buyer request a refund through PayPal, even after receiving the bitcoins, they will get their money back, no questions asked. The same principle applies to Skrill payments, even though all payments there are supposed to be "final." Opening a dispute by the buyer will, most likely, lead to a refund by Skrill.

In either scenario, the seller has lost their bitcoins, because bitcoin is a non-refundable payment method and it can't be charged back.

Dealing with bitcoin is the end-user's personal responsibility — something that should not be taken lightly. Being in full control of personal finance at any given time is both a powerful feeling and a big responsibility.

Bitcoin merchants, on the other hand, see the benefit of accepting a payment method that is not subject to chargebacks. Fraud through online payment methods is one of the biggest worries for online retailers all around the world. Bitcoin can solve that problem in its entirety. Additionally, accepting bitcoin can open the door to a new and larger customer base all around the world.

Accepting bitcoin payments in either online or offline fashion has become incredibly easy and user-friendly these days. A variety of services are at your disposal to integrate bitcoin payments buttons on your website, or even provide a way to generate bitcoin QR codes for in-store payments. This section looks at a few of the different options.

BitPay

Perhaps one of the most famous bitcoin payment processing companies is BitPay (www.bitpay.com). The company was one of the very first to embrace bitcoin payment processing and is one of the leading bitcoin payment processors in existence today.

BitPay provides a lot of benefits for both consumers and merchants willing to work with bitcoin payments. For the consumer, there are several options to send a bitcoin transaction through BitPay: You can either scan the generated QR code, copy the destination address manually, or click the in-browser link to pay directly from the bitcoin software installed on your computer.

Merchants, on the other hand, don't have much to worry about in terms of setting up BitPay integration. For website owners, a few lines of code need to be added into preexisting shopping cart systems — and that's about it. Converting the prices from local fiat currency to bitcoin is taken care of by BitPay, creating a very smooth setup experience for merchants.

As an added benefit, BitPay — as well as all other payment processors mentioned in this chapter — offer merchants the option of converting every bitcoin transaction to fiat currency on-the-fly. For most merchants, this is an important step, as their suppliers will need to be paid in fiat currency as well. Keeping in mind that bitcoin value can be quite volatile, it is a good business idea to convert the funds as soon as possible.

Unlike credit card transactions, which take up to a week to clear in the merchant's bank account, bitcoin payment earnings are received the next business day. This is a great way for merchants to stay on top of costs and earnings as well as remove any unnecessary friction between themselves and their supplies due to outstanding payments.

BitPay provides this conversion system as part of its starter package, and everything already mentioned above comes free. Once again, bitcoin is a far cheaper payment solution compared to any and all other payment methods in existence today. Plus, with no additional infrastructure to set up, no investments have to be made in order to integrate BitPay into the checkout system.

But there is more. BitPay allows merchants to accept bitcoin payments through mobile devices as well. Invoices can be generated through BitPay's mobile application, which usually results in the generation of a QR code. These QR codes include the payment address as well as the total amount to be paid. All a customer has to do is scan the QR code with their own bitcoin application, click or tap Send, and the transaction is complete. A frictionless experience for both merchants and customers alike, at no cost!

Should the need arise to upgrade the BitPay plan — for QuickBooks POS integration or VPN access, for example — there are two paid plans available as well. Both the Business and Enterprise plan offer additional functionality and features for existing BitPay customers. In the early days, the free plan will be more than sufficient for most retailers though. For more information on BitPay price plans, see `https://bitpay.com/pricing`.

Coinbase

Coinbase is another popular bitcoin payment-processing solution. Similar to BitPay (see the previous section), Coinbase offers most of the same functionalities for merchants who want to start exploring the world of bitcoin payments. Plus, Coinbase is available both in the United States and internationally, following the same path BitPay has taken over the years.

Regarding the free structure, Coinbase does things a bit differently compared to its competitors. The first $1 million worth of bitcoin transactions comes at 0 percent fee, after which a 1 percent fee will apply. Granted, for most merchants, it will take quite some time until they reach that sales figure, so there may be no reason not to choose Coinbase because of that 1 percent fee after the million-dollar mark.

Converting bitcoin to fiat currency with Coinbase takes between one and three business days to complete, depending on the merchant's location. Payments are initiated every day, however, which is still much faster than traditional payment methods such as credit cards and bank transfers.

What makes Coinbase interesting is the fact that its API offers merchants the chance to issue bitcoin refunds to the customer. In their original state, bitcoin payments are non-refundable, as already mentioned, though the recipient can manually send the money back. That same principle applies here, but in a business-esque setting. With a few clicks, merchants can refund customer transactions if they deem it necessary to do so.

More information on Coinbase for merchants can be found at `www.coinbase.com/merchants?locale=en`.

Accepting Bitcoin Payments for Your Store

Accepting bitcoin payments as a merchant or retailer takes up very little time and comes at no additional costs in terms of infrastructure.

Unlike traditional payment methods, bitcoin payments are far more user-friendly for both merchant and consumer and involve far lower transaction fees. Plus, there is no worry about having a large influx of cash payments, as bitcoin is not a physical payment option.

Online stores

Online retailers have an easy job of integrating bitcoin payments into their web stores. All it takes is a few lines of code, which are provided by the company that will process bitcoin transactions for you and which need to be added to a certain page. Once that part is complete, you can start accepting bitcoin payments without a hitch and expand your customer base on a global scale.

Most bitcoin payment processors offer e-commerce solutions for their customers and will even help in setting up bitcoin integration if needed. Additionally, most of the popular e-commerce solutions already support bitcoin integration. The reason for this is simple: no additional costs to work with bitcoin, while having every chance to attract customers from all over the world. What merchant would refuse that offer?

If an online retailer already owns a website and a domain, as most do, no additional infrastructure needs to be invested in. Bitcoin payments integrate with most major e-commerce solutions, and there are customized solutions available as well through various bitcoin payment processors (see the previous section).

Speaking of working with bitcoin payment processors, the beautiful part about accepting bitcoin transactions is that most of them will not even charge a fee for converting payments to fiat currency. Every bitcoin payment processor offers its customers the option to have (part of) every bitcoin transaction converted to fiat currency on-the-fly in order to avoid bitcoin price volatility. The converted funds are then deposited into the customer's bank account within 48 hours (two business days).

Once you have integrated bitcoin payments into your existing e-commerce solution, there is one major step left. Putting up the famous "Bitcoin Accepted Here" logo (see Figure 8-1) on your web page will alert potential customers about the payment method. Not only does this help increase bitcoin awareness on a global level, but it may also inspire others to start exploring the option of bitcoin payments as well.

Figure 8-1: Bitcoin Accepted Here . . . hurrah!

 The bitcoin checkout process for online stores is very straight-forward. All store prices — denominated in fiat currency — are converted to their respective bitcoin value during checkout by the bitcoin payment processor. On the payment page, customers see a QR code they can scan with mobile devices, and a bitcoin address to which they can manually send funds from their bitcoin software. Once the transaction has been broadcasted to the bitcoin network, the checkout process is complete.

Brick-and-mortar stores

Similar to accepting bitcoin payments online, brick-and-mortar locations do not need to invest in additional hardware if they want to accept bitcoin payments. Using a computer, smartphone, or tablet is all that is required, plus an Internet connection. Most locations have a combination of devices and Internet connectivity at their disposal, which means they can start accepting bitcoin payments within minutes.

 Just sign up with the bitcoin payment processor of your choice, which usually provides customers with a mobile application or a web interface to start accepting bitcoin payments. Installing the mobile application or setting up this web interface takes a few minutes, after which the merchant is ready for incoming payments.

Just like online payments, in-store bitcoin payment occurs through the generation of QR codes. Bitcoin payment processors allow merchants to generate a QR code with their designated BTC address and payment amount through the app or web interface.

Once the customer scans this QR code with their own bitcoin wallet — usually on a mobile device — the payment is completed within seconds.

As you may have guessed by now, accepting bitcoin through online or in-store means is very simple once the merchant gets the hang of it. In the initial stages, in-store payments require a bit of tapping on the screen before a QR code is generated. This minor learning curve is only normal when new technology arrives, and nearly all bitcoin customers will gladly lend a helping hand if needed.

Chapter 9

Staying on the Right Side of Legal

*T*hings we don't yet understand scare us, and we want to control them: aliens, the Loch Ness Monster, lawyers, and tax officials. Like those, bitcoin control can only be enforced up until a certain level. Outlawing bitcoin completely would never work simply because there is no way to monitor it properly. Despite the blockchain's transparency, wallet addresses remain pseudonymous, with no name or location attached to them.

And why would anyone want to outlaw bitcoin anyway? (Actually, check out the sidebar later in this chapter for a few ideas.)

Certain aspects of bitcoin require further investigation in order to build a regulatory framework. Using it as currency for legal purposes, such as buying and selling goods or services, is not illegal. On the other hand, most central banks have warned financial institutions and individuals about the risks associated with bitcoin, without outlawing the use of digital currency altogether.

What worries law enforcement agencies and government officials is the fact that bitcoin is not controlled by a central authority. Every bitcoin user determines the future of bitcoin, without having to bend to the will of a handful of individuals wielding the power. Decentralization is a new breed of technology that most everyday people fail to grasp properly, and that makes things occasionally, shall we say, *difficult* for bitcoin.

This chapter looks at bitcoin's legal situation in various countries and discusses what you can do to protect yourself and what you need to do to keep the taxman happy.

Understanding Bitcoin and Taxation

Daniel Defoe famously wrote, "Things as certain as death and taxes, can be more firmly believed" . . . often paraphrased as "Nothing is certain but death and taxes." I can help you with the taxes element of bitcoin, but I'm afraid you're on your own with the death bit.

Despite certain warnings issued by governments and central banks regarding bitcoin and its disruptive nature (see Chapter 1 for more on that), most countries are more than happy to allow digital currency adoption for one simple reason: taxation.

Because digital currency can be seen as an income or wage, it can be taxed. Additionally, using bitcoin to pay for goods and services is taxable in certain countries as well. As long as the government can make money from this "new breed of electronic payments," there won't be much opposition.

Remember that the regulatory tax landscape could change at any time, and it is always a good idea to check with your local government as to how bitcoin can be used, and whether or not you have to pay taxes on bitcoin. Countries such as Brazil, Canada, Finland, Bulgaria, and Denmark have issued taxation guidelines for bitcoin usage, yet not all these guidelines are in effect at the time of publication. Other countries, such as Belgium, Greece, Hong Kong, Japan, and New Zealand have no plans to tax bitcoin and other virtual currencies just yet.

Rest assured, though, that every individual country is looking into bitcoin and the impact on that country's economy. Given the decentralized and potentially global nature of the product, it may well be the case that broad regulations may have to be agreed upon at a global level before some individual countries take the plunge of determining how to regulate bitcoin as a currency, or even to treat it as a currency at all. As a practical example, many countries have their own specific laws to cover anti-money laundering and combatting the financing of terrorism (AML/CFT), and these fall under the intergovernmental organization of the Financial Action Task Force (FATF). It is possible that some intergovernmental steering will be required by some nations before they begin to issue regulations, or indeed taxation guidelines for bitcoin and other crypto-currencies within their borders. These issues aside, the need for a sovereign treasury to increase the amount collected in taxation may well be the pull factor that some countries require in order to regulate and tax bitcoin and its usage.

Taxable countries

Taxation guidelines in different countries change on a regular basis, and it is nearly impossible to provide the latest up-to-date information regarding this matter.

In Europe, things are entirely dependent on the decisions made by the European Union. In the meantime, a handful of countries have issued their own bitcoin taxation guidelines, which may be revised at a later date. The European Union will most likely not come to a decision any time soon, yet the landscape could change at any given time. Over in Asia, things are relatively quiet on the bitcoin taxation front — only Singapore is actively taxing bitcoin as a good or asset. For goods, a VAT or sales tax is applicable when buying or selling goods from local businesses using bitcoin.

The list included in this section looks at some of the countries with their own bitcoin tax laws. It was accurate at the time of writing but may have seen various changes by the time you are reading this book.

Australia

A Goods & Services Tax (GST) has been applicable to bitcoin transactions worth over AUD$10,000. However, in recent times, new regulation was proposed to treat bitcoin and other virtual currencies as "real currencies," which could lead to different taxation guidelines in the near future.

Brazil

Brazil's tax authority Receita Federal issued bitcoin taxation guidelines as follows: Digital currencies are viewed as financial assets, and are subject to 15 percent capital gains tax at the time of sale. However, bitcoin sold with a value below R$35,000 will not be subject to this taxation. Any user who holds more than R$1,000 worth of digital currencies must declare the correct amount at the end of the year.

Bulgaria

Bulgaria is one of the few European countries where bitcoin is taxable. The country's National Reserve Agency stated that the sale of digital currencies is treated as income for the sale of financial assets. As a result, a 10 percent capital gains tax is in effect in Bulgaria. Earning trades through bitcoin or other digital currencies are taxed on the same level as regular income and corporate income in the country.

Canada

Canada will be taxing bitcoins no matter what, but there are two different ways of taxing the digital currency. Bitcoin transactions used for buying and selling goods and services fall under the barter category, yet any profits made on commodity transactions are classified as income or capital.

Every bitcoin transaction is reviewed on a case-by-case basis, and any activities undertaken for profits lead to a taxpayer's income being taxed with reference to their inventory at the end of the year. Values of goods and services obtained through barter transactions must be included in the taxpayer's income, assuming they are business related.

Finland

Finland is a bit of an odd duck, as government officials imposed a capital gains tax on bitcoin and taxed bitcoin produced by mining as regular income. However, in 2014 bitcoin was classified as a commodity, as it does not meet all the proper definitions of a currency. As a result, bitcoin taxation remains confusing in Finland, so it would be best to check with a local representative.

Germany

Germany is perhaps the most advanced country in Europe, as far as bitcoin taxation guidelines are concerned. Any amount of bitcoin held for longer than a year is exempt from the 25 percent capital gains tax in effect. Bitcoin is currently considered as "private money" in Germany.

Isle of Man

The Isle of Man, a self-governing British crown dependency, is one of the few locations where an intelligent regulatory framework for digital currencies is being put in place. Exchange platforms based here need to adhere to strong Know-Your-Customer and Anti-Money Laundering regulations and Combating the Financing of Terrorism, and compliance is enforced by the Isle of Man's financial regulator, the Financial Services Authority (FSA).

Unlike most other places around the world, the Isle of Man is actively taking the necessary steps to create a regulatory framework for digital currencies. Bitcoin and other crypto-currencies do not fall within the scope of licensable activities by the island's FSA, but crypto-currency companies do need to comply with the relevant AML/CFT laws pursuant to 2015 amendments to the Proceeds of Crime Act 2008. Thus, a practical approach allows startups to register without having to go through severe licensing requirements as any self-respecting financial service regulator would enforce. This fosters an entrepreneurial culture on the island and allows the crypto-currency sector to flourish as regulations are developed over time. It is a move that will help to legitimize bitcoin in the long run, as the digital currency offers many advantages (as you will no doubt have gathered from other chapters in this book).

The Netherlands

In The Netherlands, things are very straightforward where bitcoin taxation is concerned. Bitcoin is treated like any other currency in the country, and the same taxation guidelines apply to virtual currencies as they would to regular currencies.

Slovenia

Slovenia decided not to tax the sale of bitcoins to exchanges or other community members. However, bitcoin is subject to income tax just like any regular currency in the country, and the taxation amount is calculated according to the BTC/EUR exchange rate at the time of transaction.

United Kingdom

The UK is moving forward with treating digital currencies as outside the scope of value added tax (VAT), which is a welcome move for businesses within the sector. At the time of writing, it has been announced that Jersey, another British Crown dependency, will be applying a "light touch" to regulate bitcoin in the near future. Watch this space.

United States of America

The United States is still figuring out how and whether it wants to tax bitcoin on a federal level. Due to bitcoin's unknown impact on the economy, determining a proper taxation percentage is difficult, as well as which individuals or businesses should fall into this category.

Those who receive any form of income from virtual currencies such as bitcoin should be subject to bitcoin taxation. However, this income can be divided into four different categories: wages, hobby income, bartering income, and gambling income. All of these categories are subject to different taxation percentages.

Evading taxes because you're dealing with bitcoin or other virtual currencies isn't possible. Tax evasion is one of the many situations bitcoin industry experts want to avoid by collaborating with government officials to create a proper regulatory framework.

The United States could turn out to be quite the divided front in terms of bitcoin regulation. Every state can draft its own independent laws and requirements for bitcoin users and companies alike. Some states may even decide not to regulate bitcoin altogether, depending on whether digital currency is being viewed as a currency, digital asset, or barter item.

As a result, it will take quite some time until legislators and regulators can come to an agreement as to how bitcoin usage should be regulated. Several countries have issued taxation guidelines on bitcoin already, yet the government wants to know more about the potential financial impact on local economies before taking things one step further.

Getting help with bitcoin taxes

The field of bitcoin itself is still in its early stages, and making sense of taxation guidelines in applicable guidelines is not an easy task. Luckily, there are a few services and companies helping out bitcoin users in order to calculate potential taxation amounts.

Keep in mind that not all of these services are available to every country in the world. More similar services might become available over time, although no official projects have been announced at this time.

Here are a few services and companies helping out bitcoin users in order to calculate potential taxation amounts:

- ✔ Free software called LibraTax (www.libratax.com) has integrated bitcoin support. Being able to calculate capital gains taxes and losses (for deduction) as well as getting an overview to your entire taxable bitcoin income takes just a few minutes with LibraTax. For a small fee, the company will generate a very detailed report to help you save time and money on paperwork.

- ✔ Another platform called Coyno (https://coyno.com) profiles itself as a bookkeeping solution for bitcoin users. You have the ability to import bitcoin wallets from major online service providers to create a detailed overview of incoming and outgoing transactions. At the time of writing, a proper bitcoin taxation feature was not enabled just yet, but is scheduled for release within the next 12 months.

✔ BitcoinTaxes (`https://bitcoin.tax`) serves as a platform to calculate bitcoin taxes for capital gains and income according to the latest regulatory requirements. Not only does BitcoinTaxes support bitcoin, it supports other virtual currencies such as Litecoin and Dogecoin as well. Transaction data can be imported from major exchanges or bitcoin platforms, and nearly a dozen major fiat currencies are supported at this time. There is a free plan available, which is limited to 100 transactions, whereas the paid plan (U.S. $19.95/year) includes unlimited transactions and will also import transactions from the blockchain(s) directly.

Bitcoin Regulation Around the World

Bitcoin regulation differs from country to country, just like the tax situation (see the previous section). In some countries, it may even differ from state to state, or province to province. There are no rules set in stone as far as bitcoin regulation is concerned, and some countries may even decide to never regulate bitcoin at all.

There are very few places in the world where bitcoin regulation has enforceable rules. Most countries have decided to issue a warning on bitcoin, explaining the risks to citizens in terms of bitcoin not being overseen by a central authority nor being tied to a physical asset.

Whether or not the world will be ready for the potentially disruptive technology that bitcoin brings to the table remains to be seen. Putting financial power into the sole control of the individual user rather than relying on centralized services and institutions is a major change in the world of finance.

It goes without saying that most governments and financial institutions are wary of this shift in paradigm, as they would not stand to benefit directly from mass bitcoin adoption. Even though various countries have decided to tax bitcoin, the digital currency could have a major impact on local economies, which could be either positive or negative for financial institutions.

Regulating with BitLicense

Applying existing financial regulations to bitcoin is unlikely to work, because it will most likely create an adverse effect. A prime example of such regulatory measures comes in the form of New York's BitLicense. Despite the best efforts of bitcoin industry experts, a central authority drafted rules for bitcoin companies in the state of New York that a large segment of the bitcoin community deems harsh and unreasonable.

The main concern most bitcoin companies have with the BitLicense regulation is the extensive guidelines requiring BitLicense to give customer information to the state of New York. Many bitcoin industry leaders see this as an invasion of customer privacy, leading quite a few companies to suspend services in the New York state area.

Applying for a BitLicense is subject to a $5,000 nonrefundable fee, in addition to legal costs easily ramping up to $20,000. There is no guarantee that applying for a BitLicense will be successful, and bitcoin companies may be forced to provide additional details regarding their business model or customers to state officials.

On top of that, the BitLicense regulation contains some anti-money-laundering guidelines that are in contrast with federal guidelines. To make matters worse, bitcoin companies are being scrutinized more than traditional financial institutions, which have a notorious history of fraud, corruption, and mismanagement of customer funds.

Bitcoin regulation will help legitimize the digital currency, but in our opinion BitLicense is an example of how it should not be done. The regulatory requirements put in place will hamper bitcoin growth in New York state, and the excessive costs associated with obtaining a license are just not manageable by most companies at this time.

The sum of $25,000 may not seem like much to make a business legal in the state of New York, but most bitcoin companies have a long-term picture in mind. As more and more businesses comply with BitLicense regulations, it will be seen as an incentive for other states to adopt the same guidelines. Legitimizing a bitcoin business in all 50 states combined costs in excess of $1 million.

By refusing to comply with BitLicense regulatory requirements and shutting down services in the New York state area, bitcoin companies are sending a clear message: Bitcoin regulation is a positive trend, but trying to copy-and-paste a traditional financial regulatory framework onto bitcoin companies and slapping a high price tag on license application fees will not fly.

Regulating elsewhere

Other countries around the world are not making much progress in terms of bitcoin regulation to this date. Countries such as The Netherlands and Finland have declared bitcoin to be subject to capital gains tax, but that's about as far as regulatory measures go. Both countries are sticking to a "laissez-faire" approach until the European Union comes to terms on whether or not it wants to regulate bitcoin.

Asian countries, on the other hand, are trying to prevent third-party payment processors from using bitcoin altogether. No official laws have been created declaring bitcoin to be banned or outlawed in Asian countries — with the exception of Vietnam — yet central banks are doing everything they can to discourage payment processors from getting involved with BTC.

The next few years will play a pivotal role in terms of bitcoin regulation and how it will affect mass adoption of digital currency. A healthy discussion between regulators and bitcoin industry experts would be a good place to start, but it is impossible to tell which country will allow or outlaw bitcoin in the future.

Money transmitter licenses or not?

A pressing question keeping bitcoin users on edge is whether or not their local government can classify them as money transmitters. A *money transmitter* is a business entity that provides money transfer services or payment instruments.

And after all, bitcoin can be spent, traded, and bought, making it a way of transmitting money around the world. The question to that answer is rather complex, yet some basic form of guidance seems to be in place all around the world.

Depending on where they live, individual bitcoin users may or may not be looked at as money transmitters, as long as they buy, sell, and trade bitcoin in exchange for goods and services. Once an individual starts exchanging bitcoin for fiat currency to or from other users for personal gain, a money transmitter license may be required, depending on where the user is located.

Bitcoin bans in several countries

Vietnamese government officials have officially prohibited the use of bitcoin in the country altogether. Whether or not there is an official law in place to prosecute Vietnamese citizens involved in bitcoin is uncertain, as is how severe punishment could be.

The same principle applies to Bolivia. The country's central bank, El Banco Central de Bolivia, officially banned any currency or coins not issued or regulated by the local government. This specific regulation applies to bitcoin as well as other major digital currencies such as Namecoin, Feathercoin, Dogecoin, Quark, and Peercoin. This policy issued in 2014 and officially states that "it is illegal to use any kind of currency that is not issued and controlled by a government or an authorized entity." None of the virtual currencies in existence today is issued nor controlled by a central authority, which means that Bolivia will not be dealing with digital currencies any time soon.

Colombia is another South American country that is looking to outlaw bitcoin, but it has not done so yet. Bitcoin could have a major impact on local economies, especially in countries where inflation and hyperinflation are major problems. In Colombia, it remains unclear as to whether the "ban" would be against bitcoin transactions in terms of commerce, or buying and selling bitcoin through exchange platforms, or both.

Ecuador decided to ban bitcoin completely in 2014, as well as any other form of decentralized digital currency. However, at the same time, the National Assembly of Ecuador established guidelines for the creation of its own centralized state-run currency. Government officials are permitted to make payments in "electronic money," so it will be interesting to see how this project plays out in the future.

Iceland is taking a slightly different stance on the idea of banning bitcoin. Using bitcoin as a means of transaction is not prohibited in Iceland, yet buying and selling bitcoin through foreign exchanges is not allowed. Doing so constitutes a movement of capital outside of the country, which is in violation of Iceland's capital controls.

Kyrgyzstan is not too keen on bitcoin either. The National Bank of the Kyrgyz Republic stated the use of bitcoin or other virtual currencies as a form of payment is illegal under current state law. There is only one currency deemed to be legal tender in the country, which is the som (KGS).

Other countries around the world are keeping a close eye on bitcoin to see how it could possibly impact the local economy. More countries may or may not ban bitcoin in the future, depending on how the regulatory frameworks are established across different continents.

Bitcoin enthusiasts who are involved in the mining process to generate additional bitcoins and help confirm transactions are a different matter entirely. Creating bitcoins and selling these amounts to other users for real currency or its equivalent in other commodities is in fact being a money transmitter. However, such a ruling has not been enforced anywhere in the world just yet. It is more of a sign of things to come.

Last but not least, bitcoin *exchange operators* — individuals or businesses who convert bitcoin to and from fiat currency — have to register for a money transmitter license in most jurisdictions. Regardless of whether they trade bitcoin or other virtual currencies intermittently or against fiat currency, a money transmitter license is required in almost every country of operation. One noticeable exception is that of the Isle of Man. Crypto companies in this jurisdiction have to comply with the relevant AML/CFT guidelines overseen by the island's Financial Services Authority, but their core activity is not yet licensable under current FSA guidelines.

Chapter 10

Bitcoin Security

Is bitcoin secure? One of the most often asked questions about bitcoin is whether or not the entire ecosystem is secure enough to withstand attacks from *hackers* — those people who set out to disrupt the bitcoin network in an attempt to spend their digital currency balance more than once.

The answer to that question goes way beyond a simple *yes,* and can sometimes lead to drowning in technical jargon. This chapter covers the basics, explaining whether and in what ways bitcoin is secure, and what is being done to increase the level of security as the bitcoin ecosystem grows larger.

The Bitcoin Network: An Overview of How It Works

If the mainstream media were to be believed, the bitcoin network and protocol have been hacked several times in the past few years. Nothing could be further from the truth, however. The bitcoin network itself has never been hacked successfully, nor is it ever likely to be hacked in the traditional sense.

Granted, several bitcoin users have lost coins over the course of the years, but none of that could be attributed to a flaw in the bitcoin network itself. Associated services built on top of the bitcoin network, such as exchanges and wallet providers, have become victims of poor security implementations. Once these services were breached, affected users lost their coins. Again, it had nothing to do with a flaw in the bitcoin network itself, as a decentralized network such as bitcoin cannot be "hacked."

What makes it secure

What makes the bitcoin network so secure that there is no threat from hackers to worry about? Let's take a look:

✔ The bitcoin network is decentralized, and every individual user ensures there is no central point of failure to hack the bitcoin protocol. Any individual user can become the victim of a hack, but that would have no impact on the bitcoin network. Even if all users in the United States got hacked at the exact same moment, the bitcoin network would remain intact and carry on undisturbed.

✔ The bitcoin network uses strong cryptography to guarantee the integrity and chronological order of the blockchain and all of its associated transactions. This level of cryptography can be hacked in theory, but it would take the combined processing powers of all supercomputers in existence today an unfathomable amount of years (a number with more than 15 digits, and we and our editor just don't know the right word for that number — perhaps it could just be described as a quantum leap in computing power) to have even the slightest chance at breaching the bitcoin network itself.

✔ Every individual bitcoin wallet address is protected by a private key, which needs to be provided whenever an outgoing transaction is broadcasted to the network. Users who keep bitcoin wallet software on their computer or mobile device are the sole owners of that private key, and unless their own device becomes compromised, that key cannot be discovered by anyone else in the world.

✔ The generation of new bitcoins, called *mining* (see Chapter 11 for more on mining), operates using a distributed consensus system that confirms (or rejects) transactions broadcasted to the bitcoin network through complex computational algorithms. Dedicated hardware is required to mine bitcoin successfully, and the current total amount of hardware generating additional bitcoins is still growing monthly. Plus, this is where decentralization plays a key role as well, as there are bitcoin miners all over the world. There is no option for a government to shut off the generation of new bitcoins altogether, because there is no central point of failure.

For a far more detailed explanation of the bitcoin network, check out the white paper drafted by creator Satoshi Nakamoto at `https://bitcoin.org/bitcoin.pdf`.

The role of bitcoin nodes

Individual bitcoin users are not the only driving force in terms of securing the bitcoin network. Over the past few years, dedicated bitcoin nodes have been added to the network with the sole purpose of receiving and broadcasting new bitcoin transactions to other users and nodes on the network. Doing so takes the entire decentralized aspect of bitcoin to a new level.

Every bitcoin *node* is a device — such as a computer, mobile device, or even small devices such as a Raspberry Pi 2 — that hosts the entire bitcoin blockchain since the genesis block was created in 2009. The *genesis block* was the first block of data on the bitcoin network, which awarded Satoshi Nakamoto with 50 bitcoins. Ever since that time, bitcoin users have been able to generate additional bitcoins and broadcast bitcoin transactions throughout the world.

A bitcoin node has the bitcoin client software installed, but does not receive and transfer coins on its own accord, unless the node owner decides differently. These nodes are simply additional sources where the entire blockchain is stored to verify the integrity, neutrality, and chronological order of all bitcoin transactions between the genesis block and right now. (See Chapter 7 for more on the blockchain.)

Running a bitcoin node does not reward the owner with additional bitcoins. The sole purpose of a bitcoin node is to strengthen the network. At the time of writing, there were more than 6,000 bitcoin nodes in operation, with more being added all the time. To find out more about the location of specific bitcoin nodes, visit the Bitnodes website at `https://getaddr.bitnodes.io/`.

Defending Bitcoin from Hackers

As mentioned earlier, the bitcoin network is a secure technology that is unhackable by even the strongest computers or most skilled hackers in the world. *Cryptography* — a technique for secure communication in the presence of third parties, using long sequences of unguessable secret codes — plays an important role in bitcoin's security. Properly implemented, cryptography can make a system extremely secure.

In recent years, there has been a lot of confusion in mainstream media regarding how bitcoin really works. Contrary to popular belief, bitcoin is not run by a single person or authority, and there is no such thing as the "the boss of bitcoin" or "the CEO of bitcoin." Every individual user plays an integral role in the bitcoin network, and all users are equal. And this makes it less of a juicy target for hackers.

Trying to hack the bitcoin network would be like trying to hack the Internet. There is simply no way to do it. Both bitcoin and the Internet are decentralized, with no central point of failure. Take down one part, and the network routes around the problem and continues on. The same principle applies to bitcoin.

Having no central point of failure means there is no on/off button for the bitcoin network itself. The bitcoin network spans the entire globe across all continents, and it is impossible to shut down every computer or other device connected to the bitcoin network at the same time. Not even governments could do it. Government officials may have the power to ban bitcoin usage in certain countries, but that doesn't mean the bitcoin network is not operational in those parts of the world.

Furthermore, there is no incentive to hack the bitcoin network either, because it wouldn't provide any financial benefit to hackers. All the previous network blocks include BTC that have already been distributed to other bitcoin users, and there is no chance of changing that fact. Any new coins being generated, even if the bitcoin network were to be hacked (which is all but impossible), would not go to the hackers directly either.

The bitcoin network is a technological marvel in its own right, as it provides levels of financial security we have never seen before. Despite all of that promise, there is much about the bitcoin network — and the blockchain that powers it — that we do not fully understand, and that is cause for concern. Fully comprehending the bitcoin network and its technological power will take many more years, which is why it is so important to keep growing the bitcoin community. Everyone has a different view on things and how they could be improved or potentially exploited. Preventing attacks is always better than fixing things after a successful attack.

Hacking bitcoin services

Of course, there is always the possibility of bitcoin platforms being hacked at some point. The reason for this is simple: despite being a decentralized concept, most bitcoin services or platforms (as opposed to the whole bitcoin network itself) do rely on one or more centralized servers.

By providing hackers with a target in the form of one central point of failure, shutting down a bitcoin service is far easier than attacking the bitcoin network itself. Even if a bitcoin service is breached by a hacker, there is no impact on the bitcoin network itself, as these things are not linked to each other.

Bitcoin services use the blockchain to check and handle transactions, but they are not hooked into the blockchain itself. Some people assume that if a bitcoin exchange is hacked, their connection to the blockchain makes the bitcoin network itself vulnerable as well. This is not the case, as bitcoin exchanges are services built on top of the blockchain, albeit in a centralized manner.

In fact, no direct connection exists between the bitcoin network and any bitcoin service in existence today. The only connections between users and the blockchain come from bitcoin wallets, which are in a way layered on top of the blockchain itself as well. Direct interaction and alteration of the bitcoin blockchain is impossible for individual users, which is why an individual user getting hacked does nothing to disrupt the bitcoin network at all. The same principle applies to bitcoin services being hacked, as they are a layer on top of the bitcoin network without having any direct effect on the way the network works. All bitcoin services do is broadcast certain types of transactions to the bitcoin network, but if those transactions never get relayed, the bitcoin network will continue working as before.

At its core, the bitcoin network is unaffected by anything taking place outside of its own direct reach. Only if the bitcoin network were breached and altered by 51 percent or more would there be a problem (see the next section to find out why). Given the current computational processing power securing the network, obtaining 51 percent of that amount is next to impossible for any individual or government.

On top of that, hacking bitcoin services is far more lucrative than targeting the bitcoin network itself; bitcoin exchanges, for example, store a lot of customer funds in bitcoin value, which makes it appealing for hackers to try and steal a portion of that money. Over the course of the years, many bitcoin exchanges have fallen victim to these hacks, due to poorly implemented security measures.

No matter how many bitcoin services and platforms get hacked, those situations have no effect on the blockchain itself. So long as there is at least one user running bitcoin software on any type of supported device, the blockchain will carry on and do its thing. And every day, more and more devices are running bitcoin client software to help secure the bitcoin network even more.

Watching Out for a 51 Percent Attack

One of the very few things that could do irreparable harm to the bit-coin network is the so-called 51 percent attack. To put this in simple terms (and I like simple terms as much as you do), a *51 percent attack* means that a miner or mining pool owns 51 percent of the entire bitcoin mining capacity. This could lead to a bitcoin fork, creating a secondary blockchain, which would deem any transaction on the "old" blockchain invalid.

Theorycrafting the 51 percent attack

The 51 percent attack is very unlikely to ever take place in the world of bitcoin, though it is not impossible. Once an attacker gained hold of 51 percent (or more) of the bitcoin network's computing power, he could exclude and modify the ordering of transactions for as long as he was in control of the entire bitcoin blockchain.

A 51 percent attack could have some dire consequences for the bitcoin network as a whole. For example, the person, group, or entity in charge of 51 percent of the bitcoin network would have the power to reverse transactions being sent while they were in control. Double-spending transactions — the ability to spend the same amount of bitcoin twice — would become a real issue at that time, and it would be impossible to tell which transfer was legit and which wasn't (more on this later in this chapter).

On top of that, the person or people in charge could prevent any and all transactions from getting network confirmations. Additionally, miners would be unable to mine any valid blocks on the network, with all earnings going to the people in charge, if they so desired. This is the major reason why bitcoin industry experts want to make sure a 51 percent attack can never take place under any circumstance, even though it is all but impossible to prevent.

But there are some extra points to make about this theoretical situation. One of the things the attacker(s) wouldn't be able to do is reverse bitcoin transactions from other users, because they have no control over that. Only their own transactions would be affected — yet that alone could do some major damage to the bitcoin network as a whole.

Understanding theorycrafting

Theorycraft refers to any strategy that exists only in theory and is never actually put into action.

In the bitcoin world, this means coming up with potential flaws in the network before they have been exploited. It is always a good practice to be safe rather than sorry, and bitcoin developers are working around the clock to ensure the network is safe from harm.

As technology keeps evolving, developers will have to stay on their toes and take new advancements in technology to heart. Security is an ever-evolving creature, and if proper attention isn't paid, a lot of bad things could happen. Luckily, the bitcoin developers are keeping an eye on things for us.

Preventing transactions from other users would not be possible either, as the attacker(s) would only have the power to prevent those transactions from getting any confirmations on the network. Confirmations can only occur through the generation of new blocks on the bitcoin network, and the attack(s) could shut that down completely. Furthermore, creating coins out of thin air, or even changing the number of bitcoins rewarded per block, are two major things that can't be altered either. Despite owning 51 percent of the bitcoin network's computational power, there are only so many things an attacker can affect on their own. Sending coins they never had access to is not one of those possibilities either.

Most security experts do not expect to see a voluntary 51 percent attack taking place any time soon. There is no real incentive to do so, other than having the option to double-spend coins owned by the attack(s) in charge. Without having any bitcoins in their wallet, pulling off such a successful attack would offer no monetary gain whatsoever.

How likely is a 51 percent attack?

Pulling off a 51 percent attack as an individual bitcoin miner or hacker would be nearly impossible. However, in recent years, some of the world's largest bitcoin mining pools have come close to owning 50 percent or more of the network's computational power. Due to timely changes to the affected pool, these attacks have been thwarted successfully in the past.

Ghash.io, which was one of the world's largest bitcoin mining pools a few years ago, has shown signs of an involuntary 51 percent attack on multiple occasions. The last time Ghash.io crossed the 51 percent threshold was in July 2014, forcing the bitcoin community to open a dialogue with the pool owners and the entire bitcoin mining community to come to a solution.

Temporary measures were introduced, including a pledge by Ghash.io to never exceed 29.99 percent of the entire bitcoin *hashrate* (the total computational power pointed to the bitcoin network by the miners) from that point forward. Although that amount is still fairly high for one mining pool to control, it could also be seen as a buffer against anyone trying to maliciously execute a 51 percent attack on the network.

This was the second time in less than a year Ghash.io was close to — or surpassed — the 51 percent mark of the entire bitcoin network's computational power. In January 2014, the mining pool had come close to owning 51 percent of the network as well — which resulted in the suspension of new account registrations for a longer period of time.

At the time of writing, the bitcoin network's computation network is divided across multiple mining pools. The largest mining pool at this time is China's F2pool, which holds 24 percent of the network, followed by AntPool (16 percent), BTCChina Pool (13 percent), and BW.com (10 percent). For the most up-to-date information showing actual data, check out KaikFor at `https://kaiko.com/mining`.

All the aforementioned mining pools are operated by Chinese pool operators, making China the country that owns more than half of the bitcoin network's computation power.

After the 2014 debacle, Ghash.io disappeared into obscurity as far as bitcoin mining is concerned. The overarching company, CEX.io, decided to halt all cloud mining services at the end of 2014 due to the low bitcoin price, which made it unprofitable to operate mining equipment pointed to Ghash.io. Should the cloud mining part of CEX.io be turned on again in the future, it will be interesting to see whether or not Ghash.io can reclaim some of its former glory.

Double-Spending

One major point of concern associated with bitcoin is whether or not a hacker can *double-spend* his or her coins. In theory, a double-spend could occur, and in fact it has happened. However, the risk factor associated with such an event taking place is nearly zero, because the odds are in favor of the bitcoin user or merchant. But what is a double-spend attack exactly, and how would a user be able to pull it off?

Theorycrafting the bitcoin double-spend attack

As the name suggests, a bitcoin *double-spend attack* would, technically speaking, allow one user to spend all the coins in their balance twice. For example, if someone was holding 5 bitcoin in their wallet, they would theoretically be able to spend 10 bitcoin during a double-spend scenario. However, the bitcoin network has various rules in place to prevent double-spends, making them a very rare occurrence.

Every bitcoin transaction broadcasted to the blockchain is verified by all individual nodes on the network. Every bitcoin transaction consists of an input, which is the same as the last unspent output associated with the coin balance in question. Every unspent output can only be spent once, which should make double-spending bitcoin impossible.

The race attack

Bitcoin double-spending attacks are very rare these days, yet there is always a chance someone might become a victim of a double-spend. For convenience, merchants and traders are leaning toward accepting bitcoin payments based on 0 confirmations — which leaves the door open for the same amount of coins to be double-spent by an attacker. As the transaction gains more valid network confirmations, the chances of a double-spend are shrinking exponentially.

Merchants can take several precautions to protect themselves from double-spend attacks. First and foremost, working with a bitcoin payment processor that negotiates the risk on behalf of the merchant is a step in the right direction. Most bitcoin payment processors will protect the merchant from financial harm, even when a double-spend is taking place.

Additionally, merchants and individual users can modify their bitcoin software client settings to not accept incoming connections, and only connect to trusted network nodes. Doing so all but nullifies the risk of a double-spend attack, even though waiting for at least six network confirmations is still advised at this stage.

Various types of double-spend attacks may be made against the bitcoin network. The one just discussed is called the *race attack,* which has a window of operation so long as the transaction has received no network confirmations.

Waiting for confirmations is the best remedy to ensure that a transaction is legitimate, even though this is not a feasible option for every merchant.

The Finney attack

Another popular form of double-spending attack is called the *Finney attack,* which requires the participation of a bitcoin miner once a block has been mined on the network. Precautions taken by a merchant cannot prevent the Finney attack from being executed successfully, yet a specific sequence of events must occur before the attack can be deemed a success. Overall, this method is fairly costly and can only occur every so often, making it less of a threat for merchants and service providers.

Both the Finney attack and the race attack can be combined to execute a *Vector76 attack.* In theory, this type of attack allows double-spending bitcoins even while having one network confirmation on the transaction. A successful attack would cost the attacker one block — an attacker needs to sacrifice the block by not broadcasting it to the whole network and instead relaying that block to the attacked node on the hope that they could collect the product/service before the network realized that it was an attack.

The brute force attack

Last but not least, there are the *brute force attack* and the *>50 percent attack,* both of which require an enormous amount of the bitcoin network's computational power. Neither of these types of attacks is likely at this stage, as the attacker would need to control a substantial amount of the entire bitcoin network's mining power.

The *brute force attack* works as follows:

1. The attacker submits to the merchant/network a transaction that pays the merchant, while privately mining a blockchain fork in which a double-spending transaction is included instead.

2. After waiting for *n* confirmations, the merchant sends the product.

3. If the attacker happens to find more than *n* blocks at this point, he releases his fork and regains his coins; otherwise, he can try to continue extending his fork with the hope of being able to catch up with the network. If he never manages to do this, the attack fails and the payment to the merchant will go through.

The probability of success is a function of the attacker's hashrate (as a proportion of the total network hashrate) and the number of confirmations the merchant waits for. For example, if the attacker controls 10 percent of the network hashrate but the merchant waits for 6 confirmations, the success probability is on the order of 0.1 percent.

As described in a previous section, the *>50 percent attack*, on the other hand, will only succeed if the attacker controls more than half of the network hashrate. Because the attacker can generate blocks faster than the rest of the network, he can simply persevere with his private fork until it becomes longer than the branch built by the honest network, from whatever disadvantage. No amount of transaction confirmations can prevent this attack.

The biggest threat for merchants and bitcoin service providers is a >50 percent attack, as that would indirectly make a brute force attack a guaranteed success as well. Given the current amount of computational power pointed at the bitcoin network, it seems very unlikely such an attack will ever be pulled off successfully.

One of the biggest issues with the bitcoin network is that there are too many centralized services. Nearly every bitcoin exchange and most bitcoin mining pools are centralized services. If a bitcoin exchange gets hacked, it will not affect the blockchain itself, nor open the door to double-spend attacks. But when a large mining pool gets hacked, the story could become quite different. Luckily for everyone involved, currently there is no bitcoin mining pool controlling half of the network. The largest mining pool owns about 25 percent of the entire network's computational power. However, even that percentage is sufficient to pull off a "brute force attack" in order to double-spend bitcoins, should an attacker decide to do so.

Chapter 11

Mining for Bitcoins

The concept of *bitcoin mining* revolves around the process of generating additional bitcoins until the supply cap of 21 million coins has been reached. Because bitcoins are not generated out of thin air, nor issued by a bank or government, they are generated through solving complex mathematical equations.

Without the bitcoin miners, no new coins would be brought into circulation. Though this might not be an immediate problem for most people, it would also mean that no further transactions could be confirmed on the network, which would be a much bigger worry. Without blocks being solved on the network, transactions would remain unconfirmed and could not be spent by the recipient.

But bitcoin mining is not just about generating additional bitcoins. Mining also adds transaction records to the public ledger, called the *blockchain* (see Chapter 7 for more on the blockchain). Every bitcoin transaction needs to be recorded in a block of data, and that block of data needs to be discovered by bitcoin miners. Once a transaction is included in a bitcoin block, the transaction gains one network confirmation.

Bitcoin mining has become a resource-intensive and difficult process over the past few years. As more and more people compete to mine the next bitcoin block, the difficulty rating associated with these mathematical equations is increasing steadily. By increasing the difficulty rating in this fashion, the flow of new blocks mined remains steady at about one block every ten minutes — which is why it is possible to calculate the year when the last block will be mined.

Electricity costs and investment costs to set up a proper bitcoin mining operation are quite substantial these days. Mining at home has become next to impossible, unless there is access to cheap or free electricity. This is the main reason why most bitcoin miners host hardware in China, where the bulk electricity rates are far cheaper than most places in the world.

Heading Down the Mine

No canary or gas lamp is necessary for bitcoin mining.

Mining's main purpose is to create a consensus ecosystem for bitcoin nodes to determine whether or not a broadcasted transaction is valid. As mentioned elsewhere, a minimum of six network confirmations is required to "officially" deem a bitcoin transaction spendable.

The main reason why bitcoin mining has grown increasingly resource-intensive and difficult over time is because the implemented SHA-256 algorithm makes it very difficult to calculate a block's hash. Every block hash needs to start with a certain number of zeros, meaning that quite a few attempts have to made to find the correct *solution*.

Additionally, the mining difficulty is recalculated by the network every 2,016 bitcoin blocks, and the difficulty hardly ever decreases. The difficulty factor depends on the total amount of computational power used to solve the previous 2,016 blocks on the network within a two-week period, and compensates for a rise or decline in the amount of mining power.

In the early days of bitcoin, every mined block rewarded users with the sum of 50 bitcoin. As more and more miners joined the fray, that block reward got split over miners of the pool that mined the next network block successfully. At the time of writing, the current bitcoin block reward is 25 BTC, which will be halved to 12.5 BTC a few years from now.

Bitcoin transactions are subject to a transaction fee, paid out to the miners for including that transaction in the next mined block. Although the majority of mining income is presently made up of the current block reward, those transaction fees will play a bigger role in future earnings.

Over the years, the bitcoin mining ecosystem has undergone some drastic changes. Mining now requires dedicated mining hardware to be even somewhat profitable. As mentioned, bitcoin mining is subject to high electricity fees, and the mining hardware used needs to be maintained at all times.

Addressing the variance in mining income had to take place sooner or later, which led to the creation of mining pools. Individual miners have all but disappeared from the bitcoin world, since mining through a bitcoin pool is now far more preferable. Uniting the computational power of multiple miners increases the chances of finding the next bitcoin block, and rewards are split according to the amount of computational power contributed by the individual miners.

Understanding How Bitcoin Mining Works

To recap: Unlike traditional fiat currencies, in which governments around the world can simply print more bills and mint more coins whenever they want, bitcoin has a limited supply of coins. That limit is set at 21 million, and will not be reached until 2140. Until that time, bitcoin miners use dedicated computer hardware to mine new bitcoins on the network.

As soon as bitcoin transactions are broadcasted to the network, they are picked up by miners and formed into a bitcoin block. That bitcoin block needs to be verified by the miners, and once the block has been "solved," all the included transactions are recorded in the blockchain. Every additional block discovered on the network after that stamps these transactions with one extra network confirmation.

Bitcoin miners play a key role in ensuring that the blockchain is accurate, as they take the information of a bitcoin block and verify its integrity. Afterwards, a complicated mathematical formula is applied to this block of bitcoin data, which turns the block into something different.

The "different" block consists of shorter, seemingly random sequences of letters and numbers, known in the bitcoin world as a *hash*. Hashes are easier to calculate for bitcoin miners than the full block of data, because new blocks have to be generated and mined roughly every ten minutes, and as we've said, these hashes are extremely computationally complex to solve and require expensive hardware.

Once the hash is solved, it is stored on the bitcoin blockchain, along with the block it was derived from. That process validates all transactions recorded in this bitcoin block and labels them with one network confirmation. Although the hashes are easier to solve for miners than full blocks, the increasing bitcoin mining difficulty counterbalances the scales and ensures blocks are not generated faster than ten minutes apart.

Using hashes is quite an interesting decision in its own right. This cryptographic solution is completely tamper-proof and acts as a "seal of confirmation" for the previous network block. Every hash is based on the previous block's hash, and confirms the validity of the previous block, as well as every bitcoin block coming behind it.

Given the current dedicated mining hardware being used by individuals, companies, and even hardware manufacturers, it is nearly impossible to tell how many people are actively mining right now. There is a lot of competition, as the 25 BTC reward per block is plenty of incentive to attract miners from all over the world.

Despite the increasing mining difficulty, more computational power is pointed at the bitcoin network at regular intervals. Strengthening the network not only gives miners a better chance of finding the next block — and earning bitcoin based on their share of the hard work — but also makes the bitcoin network even more secure than it already was.

Cloud Mining

Sorry, but when it comes to mining bitcoin, as we've said, operating hardware at home is now all but impossible for most everyday customers, considering electricity costs, hardware maintenance, and the noise/heat generated by dedicated hardware that has to be run in data centers. This is not possible for everyone, which is why there are companies dedicated to renting out their mining hardware for a service called *bitcoin cloud mining*.

As interesting as that terminology may sound to potential investors right now, there are both advantages and disadvantages to bitcoin cloud mining. First of all, it is important to note that not all companies offering bitcoin cloud mining are legitimate, unfortunately. Various scams have popped up, claiming to offer bitcoin cloud mining services, which turned out to be Ponzi schemes in the end. That said, there are quite a few advantages to bitcoin cloud mining, assuming you can find one of the very few legitimate companies offering that service (such as Genesis Mining, discussed shortly).

Keep in mind that profitability of bitcoin cloud mining heavily depends on the current bitcoin price, and for most cloud mining services, a bitcoin price of $320 (at current mining costs) is required to yield somewhat decent profits.

Advantages of bitcoin cloud mining

They say it takes money to make money, and that holds true for bitcoin. Getting into the bitcoin mining game without committing to some form of upfront investment is simply not possible. However, bitcoin cloud mining removes factors such as investing in bitcoin mining hardware, having it shipped to your door for a fee, and running the risk of paying VAT on top of all that.

As with any cloud service, when signing up for a bitcoin cloud mining service, you are effectively renting hardware from someone else, who purchased the machine and set up the accompanying software. There are no shipping fees involved either, because the machines are hosted by the cloud mining company itself. This cuts down tremendously on the upfront investment costs, depending on your location, of course.

But there is still an investment to make when signing up for bitcoin cloud mining services. Most companies will offer yearly or lifetime contracts to their customers, and these companies will mine bitcoin on your behalf for the agreed period of time. A price tag is attached to these contracts, which varies from provider to provider.

In exchange, you as a customer will be up and running with bitcoin cloud mining within a few minutes of completing your order. There are no settings to worry about, as nearly every bitcoin cloud mining provider will automatically point your rented hardware to a bitcoin mining pool. Earnings will start trickling in slowly, and depending on which provider you sign up with, waiting on a return of income can be either brief or it can take a while.

With no shipping costs and VAT risk to take into account, bitcoin cloud mining seems to be a safe bet when it comes to entering the mining scene. The wait for a return on investment, let alone profit, is a factor to take into account, as it depends on multiple factors — the bitcoin price, for one, but also the mining difficulty, which changes every 2,016 blocks, and the overall computational power aimed at the bitcoin network in general.

Disadvantages of bitcoin cloud mining

If there are advantages in using a certain service, you can be sure that there will also be disadvantages . . . and there are quite a few disadvantages to bitcoin cloud mining.

As a customer, with cloud mining you're never in full control of the hardware you rent, because you cannot physically or remotely access the miner itself. You rely on a centralized third-party service provider to be honest with you and not to pocket a share of earnings for itself. This is where most of the issues surrounding bitcoin cloud mining start, as customers feel they are not being paid out correctly. There are several reasons for payments to seem short, and some of those reasons might even be legitimate. Unexpected maintenance costs for hardware, a supplier upping their prices, electricity costs changing, and the ever-changing bitcoin price are just a few potential causes.

Then again, there is no way to verify the truth of why the mining earnings might be reduced for a certain period. Customers being forced to rely on a third-party service provider is exactly what bitcoin set out to change by giving every individual user full control at any time.

Another disadvantage of bitcoin cloud mining is the maintenance and electricity fees. Even though you don't host the hardware at your place, where you would pay these costs, the bitcoin cloud-mining operator does have to pay them, and those charges are passed along to you. These dedicated machines are not really floating in the clouds, of course. They're physically hosted in a real location and need to constantly be fed electricity to operate. In some parts of the world, such as China, electricity is relatively cheap, which makes these fees less substantial.

The biggest misconception most people have about bitcoin cloud mining is the fact they will buy a certain amount of computational power and earn the full reward of that power. This is never the case, as electricity and maintenance costs will be calculated based upon how much computational power you are "renting" from the service provider.

Bitcoin cloud mining can still be profitable for smart investors, assuming they have done their research and calculations themselves. Never rely on the project earnings given to you by a cloud mining service operator, as there are too many variables to influence that outcome. Plus, there are quite a few mining profit calculators out there who will project a completely different — and lower — earnings number, but at least they are far more realistic in their calculations.

Risks associated with bitcoin cloud mining

Perhaps the biggest risk associated with bitcoin cloud mining is coming across a service provider that looks legitimate but is not. Most bitcoin cloud mining companies will offer to show you pictures of their mining farms, which, of course, may or may not be real.

Added to that, whenever a bitcoin cloud mining company gets hacked — and that does happen quite frequently — customer earnings are affected as well. User funds tend to go missing, and the service provider is forced to reduce mining earnings for an extended period of time to recoup losses.

One confirmed legitimate bitcoin cloud mining company is Genesis Mining (www.genesis-mining.com). This Hong Kong company has been active in the bitcoin cloud mining business since 2013, and it offers lifetime mining contracts at affordable prices. Unlike most other companies, there are no extra or hidden fees associated with purchasing a bitcoin cloud-mining contract from Genesis Mining, making it the preferred service provider for miners.

If you purchase a cloud-mining contract at some point, keep in mind that the next best offer might just be around the corner. The bitcoin cloud-mining scene is constantly evolving, adjusting, and becoming more competitive. Always do your own research, check out the various offerings, and make a well-educated decision. Don't get swayed by offers that seem too good to be true, as they usually are.

Securing Bitcoin with Mining

The bitcoin network is only as strong and secure as the people supporting it either by running a bitcoin node or by dedicating computational power to the mining process.

As discussed in Chapter 10, one of the things posing a threat to the bitcoin network is the so-called 51 percent attack. More computational power pointed to the mining process reduces the chances of malicious individuals managing to obtain 51 percent of the network power and doing harm to bitcoin.

From a miner's perspective, of course, the monetary gain is the most obvious incentive to dedicate powerful mining hardware to this process. However, there are also miners who do this "job" for the benefit of making the bitcoin network more secure and see the monetary gain as an added bonus for doing so. Regardless of which side of the fence they are on, mining secures the bitcoin network by confirming transactions and moving the blockchain along.

But there is more to it than that. Mining also protects the neutrality of the network by preventing one individual or mining pool from gaining the power to block other transactions. As Chapter 10 explains, anyone who gains that much computational power can only confirm their own network blocks, and leave other transactions unconfirmed by an undetermined amount of time.

Bitcoin mining makes it increasingly difficult for any individual or mining pool to reverse a previous transaction, because all blocks following this transaction will need to be rewritten. Every network block gains additional confirmation as more time progresses, which is why it is pivotal to keep the blockchain going and generate new blocks roughly every ten minutes.

Bitcoin mining is designed to be very resource-intensive and to become even more so as time progresses. Every individual block found on the network requires a certain proof-of-work to be deemed valid, which is then further verified by all the bitcoin nodes on the network. Once these nodes receive a tamper-proof consensus, new coins will be disseminated in a decentralized manner, motivating miners to keep pointing resources to the bitcoin network. More resources means a higher level of security, and this cycle continues to repeat itself.

Starting Your Own Mine

Getting involved in the bitcoin mining game is now more difficult than it used to be. Mining hardware has evolved at an accelerated rate in recent years, as the mining difficulty ramped up and demanded more intensive computational hardware to solve blocks. But there are still ample opportunities to get involved with bitcoin mining, assuming you have substantial resources and carefully do some calculations beforehand.

Getting the right hardware

When bitcoin was released in 2009, the mining process was quite simple. All a user had to do was install the bitcoin software client, let it synchronize with the bitcoin network, and make sure the checkbox on the Mining tab was checked. Any type of CPU inside a computer — even laptops — could be used to mine bitcoins, because there was next to no competition on the network. In fact, during the first few weeks, there were only a handful of miners.

It didn't take long for a bitcoin enthusiast to figure out the code to let his graphics card do all the computational work, as graphics cards are designed to do exactly that. Even when playing video games, a graphics card is doing nothing more than processing computational data over and over again, at a rapid pace.

 The difference in mining speed between CPU mining and GPU mining is simply astonishing. Productivity increases exponentially, and the first GPU miners started strengthening the bitcoin network tenfold. Despite all that extra mining power, new blocks were still ten minutes apart, thanks to the change in mining difficulty.

A few years ago, CPU and GPU mining became completely obsolete when FPGAs came around. An *FPGA* is a Field Programmable Gate Array, which can produce computational power similar to most GPUs around 2013, while being far more energy-efficient than graphics cards. Needless to say, quite a few miners switched from CPU mining to GPU mining and then to FPGA mining within a few years.

But the mining hardware business keeps evolving even now, and FPGAs were only useful for a short amount of time. Bitcoin ASICs were introduced to the scene in 2013, and these Application-Specific Integrated Circuits cut down electricity requirements even further, while outperforming GPU and FPGA mining by quite a margin.

That said, there are some downsides associated with bitcoin ASIC mining. Although the energy consumption is far lower than graphics cards, the noise production goes up exponentially, as these machines are far from quiet. Additionally, ASIC bitcoin miners produce a ton of heat and are all air-cooled, with temperatures exceeding 150 degrees F.

Buying a bitcoin ASIC miner also involves some hefty shipping fees — these machines are quite heavy. Plus, you are guaranteed to pay import duty on a bitcoin ASIC shipment as well, due to the size and weight. All in all, ASICs today are a very costly investment with absolutely no guarantee of the customer ever breaking even, let alone making a profit.

Last but not least, bitcoin ASICs can only produce so much computational power until they hit an invisible wall. Most devices are not capable of producing more than 1.5 TH/s (terrahash) of computational power, forcing customers to buy these machines in bulk if they want to start a somewhat serious bitcoin mining business.

It should come as no surprise to find out that most people have moved away from bitcoin mining hardware themselves and switched over to cloud mining (even though there are a lot of risks associated with bitcoin cloud mining companies, as most of them are far from legitimate.) And the low bitcoin price is not helping matters either. See the earlier section on cloud mining to find out about the measures you can take to protect yourself.

Calculating your costs

Regardless of whether you want to buy hardware or sign up for a bitcoin cloud-mining contract, you need to do some homework to determine costs, earnings, and the expected time until you receive your investment back to start making a profit.

 Bitcoin mining costs go far beyond the original investment in the hardware, logistics costs, and import duty fees. One of the main factors to keep in consideration is power usage, as electricity costs fluctuate greatly from country to country.

 In most countries, the price per kilowatt hour (kWh) makes bitcoin mining unprofitable. Make sure to check a recent electricity bill and determine the price per kWh and then calculate how much kWh your bitcoin mining hardware will use on a daily basis.

For example, a bitcoin miner drawing 600 watts from the wall will consume 12.4 kWh per day. Calculations for this are simple: 600W × 24 hours in a day = 12,400W or 12.4 kWh. If you pay $0.10 per kWh, your daily electricity bill will be $1.24.

 This cost has to be weighed against the daily income you can earn from bitcoin mining. These daily earnings will heavily depend on the current bitcoin price, which is fairly low at the time of writing. A higher bitcoin price would drastically improve earnings, while electricity costs remain the same (unless your supplier decides to make a price change).

 Electricity is not the only cost. Owning bitcoin mining hardware means maintaining it at all times and repairing it if something breaks down. Some bitcoin ASIC miners don't come with a power supply, which you have to purchase as well.

The biggest and most important cost is investing time and effort to optimize mining earnings. Most bitcoin mining hardware will per-form at its highest rate out of the box, but there are always tweaks that can be made. Most manufacturers release new firmware for the mining hardware at regular intervals to fix any bugs and squeeze out that extra bit of computational power.

Using a profitability calculator

Luckily, calculating your costs and potential earnings doesn't require a math degree, or even a pen and paper. Several websites specialize in providing accurate mining profitability calculations. You simply enter various hardware information and electricity costs.

Keep an eye on these mining-profitability calculation websites. They will not only give you an estimate for mining today, but also for the foreseeable future. The bitcoin mining difficulty adjusts every 2,016 blocks, which affects your mining earnings as well. If the difficulty increases, your earnings will go down slightly, whereas earnings increase if the mining difficulty decreases.

To find bitcoin mining profitability calculators, simply search online for "bitcoin mining profitability calculator."

Part IV
The Part of Tens

Check out an extra Part of Tens chapter at www.dummies.com/extras/bitcoin.

In this part . . .

✔ Check out ten great ways to use bitcoin.

✔ Find out about some other interesting alternative currencies.

✔ Explore ten online bitcoin resources.

Chapter 12

Ten Great Ways to Use Bitcoin

*B*itcoin can be used in so many different ways, and the only real limits are its current restricted acceptability in terms of a payment solution. As it grows in popularity and acceptance by more merchants, you should be able to use it for purchasing whatever you like. Hoorah!

Whether you want to use bitcoin as a form of virtual currency education, use it as an extra income, or look at it from an investment perspective, bitcoin allows you to do just about anything you can possibly imagine. This chapter suggests ten of the best ways to use bitcoin, even though there are many, many more options at your disposal.

Use Bitcoin as an Investment Vehicle

Most people see bitcoin as an investment for the future. With its limited supply cap of 21 million coins (expected to be reached in 2140) and the current low bitcoin price, there are ample opportunities to make a quick profit from investing in bitcoin.

Trying to play the bitcoin price market is absolutely fine by us, but keep in mind that financial losses often come quicker than profits.

Other forms of using bitcoin as an investment vehicle exist as well. Investing in bitcoin can be a part of a long-term plan, rather than an attempt at quick profits and losses. Bitcoin is still in the very early stages of development, having been around for only six years. There is still a long way to go in terms of educating people on bitcoin, which creates an investment opportunity in its own right.

Use Bitcoin As An Educational Tool

The main purpose of bitcoin, as we see it anyway, has always been to educate people on the potential of the blockchain and how to take back full control of their lives, not just from a financial perspective, but also in the way people use services, platforms, technology, and more importantly, how they look at the world.

Everywhere you look, you'll find fraud, corruption, mismanagement, financial restrictions, limited free speech, and many other things that should not be issues in this day and age. When Satoshi Nakamoto created bitcoin, the idea was not only to create a new breed of disruptive technology, but also to show everyday people that there are solutions available to decentralize our entire lifestyle and avoid such nastiness as fraud and corruption.

 Up until now, most of bitcoin's focus has been on the price and the financial aspect of the technology. There's a lot of room for improvements in this market, and bitcoin is a fun tool to explain to people how the financial system can — and perhaps should — be changed.

But it goes much further than that, as bitcoin's educational prowess extends beyond finance and technology. The potential of blockchain technology and bitcoin 2.0 is wide-reaching, as discussed in Chapter 7. Once you understand the functionality of bitcoin and the blockchain, dear reader, you will also be free to think about its potential in other aspects of everyday life. Think for a moment, for example, how majority consensus could be reached, even without having to rely on the human element in the equation. Digital voting, negotiating and amending contracts, signing and storing documents, and revamping the peer-to-peer way of transacting are just a few examples of bitcoin's educational potential through unleashing the potential of the blockchain.

Go and Spend Bitcoin for Everyday Needs

Bitcoin is an electronic form of payment, which is one of the many reasons so many people are attracted to this virtual currency. Over the past few years, more and more places have started accepting bitcoin payments as an alternative form of payment due to lower costs, instantaneous transactions, and no risk of fraud or chargebacks.

As a result, bitcoin is becoming a viable form of payment, both online and in-store at various locations throughout the world. The bitcoin ecosystem is mostly used for sending funds around the world, which also means that commerce is a major factor in keeping the ecosystem alive.

With so many different merchants to choose from — some of which can even be used for everyday goods and services — bitcoin is slowly becoming a mainstream form of payment.

One interesting option to spend bitcoin comes in the form of services and companies that deliver food to your doorstep. Or, if you are a huge Starbucks fan, why not use bitcoin to buy your next coffee? The possibilities are endless.

A quick Internet search shows you more ways of spending bitcoin than you ever thought possible at this stage. If you're searching online for info on spending bitcoin, try using the following keywords:

- ✔ "Spend bitcoin"
- ✔ "Use bitcoin"
- ✔ "Pay with bitcoin"
- ✔ "Bitcoin accepted here"

Indulge in Luxury Expenses with Bitcoin

Bitcoin has managed to attract people from all different walks of life. While giving these people the opportunity to become part of a new breed of financial ecosystem, bitcoin can also be used for less frequent purchases, such as flights and hotel bookings. Even though not every flight or hotel can be paid in bitcoin just yet, multiple services are at your disposal to facilitate the process, such as BTCtrip (https://btctrip.com).

One interesting phenomenon these companies have noticed is how bitcoin customers are willing to spend slightly more on their flights and hotel bookings. It could be that bitcoin users are more comfortable spending larger amounts on travel, or perhaps they were just offered unfavorable exchange rates at the time. The exact reason for this remains a mystery to this very day, but it just goes to show that bitcoin acceptance is beneficial to both merchants and consumers, regardless of what product or service they offer.

Support Charities with Bitcoin

One of the most important aspects of life is having the opportunity to do social good for other people who need it the most. Bitcoin donations can be sent to various charitable organizations, including the Red Cross and Greenpeace. In fact, some charities will even help you with deducting the donation from your yearly taxes, even though the payment was made in bitcoin.

The biggest advantages bitcoin brings to the table, in terms of charity, is how you can send funds directly to the people in need, rather than having to rely on third-party organizations. During the Nepal earthquake disaster, for example, many bitcoin enthusiasts sent donations directly to the Nepal Relief Fund, rather than going through the charity in their country. As a result, more funds made their way to the affected area faster, and bitcoin users managed to help lots of people in the affected region.

Gamble Online

Depending on where you're located, online gambling and sports betting may or may not be legal, so make sure to check with your local laws and regulations first.

If online gambling *is* legal where you are, bitcoin offers a great alternative payment method compared to credit cards and bank transfers. No personal details are required, and no verification documents — simply deposit funds and start playing. Bitcoin transfers are fast and nonrefundable, making them a perfect payment method for online service providers such as casinos.

Now, we know you're a sensible, responsible grown-up, but we do just want to remind you to gamble responsibly. Lecture over!

Invest in Precious Metals: The Gold Standard Reinvented

Although this is technically the same as looking at bitcoin as an investment vehicle, very few people know that bitcoin can be used to purchase precious metals, such as gold and silver.

On top of that, various online platforms let users trade bitcoin against the value of precious metals as a form of day trading, some of whom have seen some great success over the years. Always do your own research before trusting just any platform though.

Vaultoro (`www.vaultoro.com`) is by far the most popular online platform at the time of writing (focusing mostly on gold and bitcoin.) Others include MidasRezerv (`https://midasrezerv.com`), Uphold (`https://uphold.com`), and BitGold (`https://bitgold.com`). Always do due diligence and look up the companies and their reputations before investing any bitcoin.

Give It Away! The Joy of Gifting Bitcoin

In the words of the Red Hot Chili Peppers, "Give it away, give it away now!" They may not have been singing about bitcoin (so far as we know), nevertheless bitcoin is a perfect gift for friends, family, and loved ones.

Several sites offer gift cards in exchange for bitcoin as well, such as Gyft (`https://gyft.com`) and eGifter (`https://egifter.com`). Bitcoin is usable for this through many merchants, most of which do not even accept bitcoin payments directly. But through the magical power of gift cards, bitcoin can be spent or gifted as a payment method.

Pay Bills

The option of paying bills with bitcoin depends on where you live. That said, there are multiple platforms in development that will let you pay any bill with bitcoin in exchange for a small commission.

Phone bills, utility bills, and mortgage bills will be paid in bitcoin in the not-so-distant future. Mobile phone top-ups through bitcoin payments have been possible for quite some time now, though this functionality is not available worldwide just yet.

Use Bitcoin as a Social Experiment

Let's assume you are very passionate about bitcoin but find its current lack of usability rather disheartening. Why not go out and try to convince merchants and consumers about the benefits of bitcoin? After all, growing the ecosystem one step at a time takes time and effort, and since there is no centralized authority to take care of the job, every bitcoin community member has some responsibility to push bitcoin adoption.

All these are just a fraction of the possibilities you can experience with bitcoin, and coming up with your own creative ways to use the virtual currency is of great value to the community. Whenever you have a chance to use bitcoin, make sure to share your story with the community.

Chapter 13

Ten (or So) Other Crypto-Currencies

● ●

In This Chapter

▶ Trading between crypto-currencies

▶ Peeking inside the coin community

▶ Gambling and crowdfunding

● ●

*T*he world of digital currencies is teeming with eager developers who feel they can create the "next bitcoin." Over the years, a few thousand *altcoins* have been released, and most have disappeared into obscurity because they were nothing more than pump-and-dump schemes to make a quick profit. But there are a few altcoins besides bitcoin in existence that are of some importance, even though they will not dethrone bitcoin any time soon.

This chapter looks at the eight digital currencies that have different twists. (To build this up to a full list of ten, we wanted to add bitcoin twice, because we think it's twice as good, but our editor wouldn't allow it. So we'll stick with eight.)

Litecoin: The Silver to Bitcoin's Gold

Perhaps the most widely known altcoin is Litecoin (https:// litecoin.org), which uses an entirely different algorithm (Scrypt) from bitcoin's (SHA-256). Litecoin was the first altcoin to use the Scrypt algorithm, which gave bitcoin miners a reason to hold onto their outdated GPU hardware and generate income by pointing their hardware to mine Litecoin instead.

Litecoin has managed to stay relevant for an extended period of time, simply because it was the first of its kind to try and do something new. That initial ideology led to the creation of a significant

Litecoin community, which has remained loyal and faithful throughout the years.

The only additional advantage to Litecoin, besides utilizing GPU for mining, is that the mining time between blocks is five minutes, compared to ten minutes for bitcoin.

Most of Litecoin's success can also be attributed to all the crypto-currency exchanges listing Litecoin trading pairs, and effectively creating secondary trading markets. In fact, Litecoin can be traded on pretty much all crypto-currency exchanges in existence today, although only a handful of exchanges offer a Litecoin/fiat currency trading option. Various payment processors have added Litecoin to their repertoire of coins as well, giving the community a way to spend LTC in most places where bitcoin is accepted as well.

Many of the altcoins available today are based on Litecoin's Scrypt algorithm.

Dogecoin: Such Wow, Much Fun, Very Coin

When Dogecoin (http://dogecoin.com) was launched, it seemed to be a "meme" coin, as it was presented in a very cartoon-ish way. With no hard coin supply cap, and taking a page from Litecoin's book by using the Scrypt algorithm, no one expected Dogecoin to become a major crypto-currency.

Lo and behold, the third largest crypto-currency community in the world will gladly tell you otherwise. Dogecoin prides itself upon being a *community crypto-currency*, which resulted in various community efforts to raise funds for good causes.

Two achievements of raising funds with Dogecoin have included getting the Jamaican bobsled team to the 2014 Sochi Winter Olympics and raising funds for Josh Wise to participate in the number 98 car in Talladega Superspeedway NASCAR May 2014 race.

Dash: Formerly Known as Darkcoin

Throughout this book, you may notice how the topic of anonymity keeps coming back. Bitcoin in itself does not offer anonymity per se, but rather *pseudonymity*, as users can mask their identities with a wallet address. This lack of anonymity has allowed various altcoin developers to come up with potential solutions to this problem, and features have been developed that may, or may not, make their way to bitcoin software in the future.

Darkcoin, or Dash (https://dash.org) as it is called these days, is one of the frontrunners on the topic of developing anonymity features. Evan Duffield, the main Dash developer, has come up with several creative solutions to create fully autonomous and anonymous transactions over the Dash network. Dash continues to be one of the more popular anonymity altcoins.

Ripple: A Different Type of Crypto-Currency with Potential

Nearly every crypto-currency you will ever encounter embraces the ideology of decentralizing life as we know it. Ripple (https://ripple.com) is slightly different, as it was created and is maintained by Ripple Labs. Based on market capitalization, Ripple is one of the largest crypto-currencies in existence today.

Ripple is getting quite a lot of media attention at the time of writing. Its protocol has been implemented by Fidor Bank and other payment networks as settlement infrastructure technology. According to some banks, Ripple's technology of distributed ledgers has a number of advantages over bitcoin's blockchain technology, including security and price.

Peercoin: Introducing Proof-of-Stake

Bitcoin and Litecoin have one thing in common: New coins can only be generated through the mining process. Peercoin (https://peercoin.net) was one of the first "bitcoin clones" to offer a new system to generate coins, called *proof-of-stake*. The way proof-of-stake works is by having an amount of coins sitting in your wallet for a certain period, without spending them.

Once these coins reach a certain *age* — a period during which they have not been moved — they generate a small interest percentage. The whole principle works in the same way as a bank's savings account, but in a completely decentralized manner, with the user being in full control of their funds at all times.

Allowing the generation of additional Peercoins through proof-of-stake also provides an additional layer of network stability, as the numbers of miners may decline over time, but there will always be users staking their PPC. Additionally, Peercoin developers have implemented a steady inflation rate of 1 percent per year, with no hard coin supply cap put in place.

StartCOIN: Crowdfunding

StartCOIN is all about crowdfunding and is reward-based. The coin rewards users who pledge, share, and hold StartCOIN on a dedicated website titled StartJOIN (https://startjoin.com).

Crowdfunding has gained popularity, which StartCOIN has taken advantage of by allowing communities to fund ideas, concepts, and projects. Those who pledge or gain funding via the website then are also rewarded with StartCOINs as an additional incentive.

NXT: Using Proof-of-Stake for Transaction Consensus

Unlike bitcoin's consensus through mining, NXT (http://nxt.org) uses proof-of-stake to reach a transaction consensus. Additionally, NXT is one of the very few crypto-currencies that has no mining process — all coins were distributed during the launch of this altcoin. Having a steady supply of coins, available at any given time, created a new ecosystem in the world of crypto-currency.

What makes NXT truly interesting is the fact that any user can create their own crypto-currency within the NXT ecosystem. All newly created coins are backed by NXT currency and can be distributed in a variety of ways.

In more recent times, NXT has gradually introduced new features such as smart contracts, an arbitrary messaging service, and a proper decentralized peer-to-peer exchange platform called MultiGateWay.

CasinoCoin: Branding for Casino Users

One coin that is now starting to see the benefit of having a good name behind it is CasinoCoin (`http://casinocoin.org`). Given the name, it should be obvious that it is related to the casino marketplace.

CasinoCoin has positioned itself using the same technology as Litecoin (the Scrypt algorithm), but by having a brand name, it allows the public to understand immediately the affiliation of the coin and where its target user is.

Chapter 14

Ten Online Bitcoin Resources

In This Chapter

▶ Delving for more information and knowledge

▶ Checking the news online and through regular media

▶ Keeping up with the latest bitcoin trading news

*F*inding out more information about bitcoin, the blockchain, and how the digital currency is evolving can also be done away from the pages of this book, believe it or not.

Quite a few resources are at your disposal, all of which are aimed to bring you up-to-date information on the bitcoin ecosystem. This chapter gives you ten of the most common news sources for the most up-to-date bitcoin info.

The Bitcoin Wiki

Having an unbiased and independent source of bitcoin information is a valuable asset to the virtual currency community, because there are constant changes, updates, and new services popping up. One of the most commonly used sources for information on the Internet is Wikipedia, and bitcoin has its own subsection explaining all of the terminology in finer detail.

On the bitcoin wiki, you can find all sorts of information, ranging from info about creator Satoshi Nakamoto — even though he remains quite a mystery — to mining, running a bitcoin node, and much, much more. Definitely a source to keep an eye on, as there is always something to learn about bitcoin you didn't know yet.

Check it out here: `https://en.wikipedia.org/wiki/Bitcoin`.

BitcoinTalk Forums

One of the most popular places for bitcoin debates and service reviews is bitcointalk.org. These forums, dedicated to bitcoin and created many years ago, are home to breaking news, project development, services and goods, and much more. If there is anything regarding bitcoin you want to have a healthy discussion about, the BitcoinTalk forums are a must-visit.

That being said, not everything posted on the BitcoinTalk forums is bitcoin-related, mind you. A dedicated section for alternate virtual currencies, including Litecoin, Dogecoin, and others, is available as well. Plus, there are special subforums for specific popular languages, including Dutch, French, Russian, and Chinese.

Check it out here: `http://bitcointalk.org`.

Bitcoin subReddit

Avid users of Reddit may already have stumbled upon the bitcoin subReddit at some point in their online browsing careers. The bitcoin subReddit is home to many discussions that can touch upon a variety of subjects: taking bitcoin to space and why payment processors are charging so few fees on transactions. Many more debates are opened and closed on a daily basis there.

There is a downside to the bitcoin subReddit as well. At the time of writing, censorship is plaguing this platform at an alarming rate, and moderators often ban people and remove topics.

However, all in all, the bitcoin subReddit is still a good place from an information point of view, even if the overall community reaches toxic levels every now and then.

Check it out here: `http://reddit.com/r/bitcoin`.

Bitcoin.org (and bitcoin.com)

For the most part, bitcoin.org has been the "home page" of bitcoin on the Internet. A brief explanation of bitcoin, along with a few demo videos and wallet software download links, is what this portal is all about. Providing information in a useful and convenient manner, without overwhelming novice users, this website is a great way to present bitcoin to the outside world.

One of the most common searched terms — when it comes to finding out more information about bitcoin on Google and Bing — is "bitcoin.com". Until a few months ago (at the time of writing), bitcoin.com was a domain redirecting to an entirely different website and only recently became a portal for all things bitcoin. In addition, and unlike bitcoin.org, bitcoin.com has added a news section, which is updated daily with fresh content and opinionated pieces.

Check them out here: `http://bitcoin.org` and `http://bitcoin.com`.

Bitcoin News Sites and Blogs

Any type of trend or niche would not remain relevant without a few dedicated news sites covering everything about the subject matter. In the case of bitcoin, quite a few news blogs are out there, most of which are run as hobby projects and therefore are only updated every now and then. Bitcoin is still fairly new, and there is a lot of room for competition in the news scene.

That being said, there are also dedicated bitcoin news outlets. Bitcoin magazine, Inside Bitcoins, CoinDesk, Bitcoinist, bitcoin.com, and CoinTelegraph are the most popular ones. Every news site tries to cover news in a completely different way, providing users with multiple angles on the same stories quite regularly. The beautiful thing about bitcoin is that everyone who is an active writer has their own take on things, and connecting seemingly random events makes the entire ecosystem so interesting.

Check them all out here:

- ✔ `http://bitcoinmagazine.com`
- ✔ `http://insidebitcoins.com/news`
- ✔ `http://coindesk.com`
- ✔ `http://bitcoinist.net`
- ✔ `http://bitcoin.com`
- ✔ `http://cointelegraph.com`

Mainstream Media

Even though mainstream media have a habit of putting bitcoin in a negative spotlight, there's more coverage on the topic of virtual currencies than ever before. And it's growing.

The underlying technology is of great value to financial institutions and innovative companies, whereas bitcoin as a currency can help citizens legally bypass capital controls enforced by governments.

Although most of the bitcoin focus remains negative, mainstream media is keeping a close eye on the progression made by virtual currencies. More and more people are aware of bitcoin, and mainstream media outlets will have to keep up with this trend if they want to remain relevant.

Bitcoin Documentaries

Over the years, multiple bitcoin documentaries have been created, following the history of this disruptive virtual currency so far. Nearly all of these documentaries can be found online and are free to watch. The main reason for putting together a bitcoin documentary seems to be not to make money, but to create a visual medium for everyday consumers to see and experience how bitcoin can, and will, change the world, one step at a time.

By the time you are watching these documentaries, some of the information will be slightly out of date (sad but true, the same also applies to sections of this book, but that's why we've included this section, you see). However, these videos will likely withstand the test of time, as they all document the struggles and uphill battles bitcoin enthusiasts had to overcome.

Check out the best ones here:

- ✔ http://bitcoinfilm.org/documentaries/
- ✔ www.coindesk.com/six-bitcoin-documentaries-watch/

Bitcoin Price Charts

Bitcoin is about more than just the current exchange price, but a lot of people want to focus their attention on keeping up to date with the current bitcoin value. There are various sites where you can see the current bitcoin price, the average trading volume, and charts distinguishing between buy and sell orders.

BitcoinWisdom is one of the most often-used sites. It aggregates data from various exchanges around the world, broken down across major fiat currency trading pairs. All information is free to use and updated in real time (as far as the exchange APIs allow for that update frequency).

There is also Coinmarketcap.com, which shows the current market capitalization for all virtual currencies in existence today.

Check them out here:

✔ `http://bitcoinwisdom.com`

✔ `http://coinmarketcap.com`

FiatLeak

For those who don't like to look at boring financial charts all day, FiatLeak.com is a fun way to see real time buying action. FiatLeak gives a visual representation of live bitcoin buy orders. Bitcoin symbols fly all across the world map shown on this website, indicating which country is responsible for the largest trading volume at any given moment.

Watching this website is quite fun and mesmerizing at the same time — there is a lot more bitcoin trading going on than you might expect. The amount of bitcoin being traded across the world is simply amazing, and FiatLeak gives you a great visualization of where the funds are coming from and going to.

Check it out here: `http://fiatleak.com`.

CoinMap and CoinATMRadar

If you're ever wondering where you can find a bitcoin ATM, to both buy and sell bitcoin in a convenient way in exchange for fiat currency, look no further than CoinATMRadar. On this website you can see a frequently updated list of bitcoin ATMs all around the world. In fact, there are more of these machines than one might think, even if they are far from being as common as regular bank ATMs.

CoinMap, on the other hand, gives a worldwide overview of places where bitcoin can be spent in-store. Depending on where you live, the number of locations might be fairly limited, but more places will be added over time. CoinMap relies on information provided by the community to keep these maps up to date, so if you know of places where bitcoin can be spent, make sure to submit them.

Check them out here:

✔ `https://coinmap.org/#/map/`

✔ `http://coinatmradar.com`

Index

About the Author

Prypto was established in 2013 to innovate simple and effective bitcoin-related solutions, with its first product being the Crypto Scratch Card. This allows users to first experience crypto-currencies through physically having their hands on a scratchcard. The company's products have reached all corners of the globe and have allowed people to be introduced to bitcoin through their easily accessible solutions.

Just as this book aims to demystify bitcoin and the blockchain technologies underpinning it, Prypto's company aim is to simplify access to the blockchain for businesses both large and small by providing bespoke solutions that can be tailor-made. The company will be rolling out different products that showcase the potential of the blockchain in a way that is understandable and allows businesses to take their first steps into integrating this new technology and opening up exciting real-world applications.

Prypto is proud to be the author of *Bitcoin For Dummies* and believes that the more the methods of what bitcoin and associated technology bring are understood, the better for everyone. We are firm believers in the potential good that can come about through the evolution of bitcoin and the blockchain and hope that you can share some of our excitement as we move forward.

Authors' Acknowledgments

Thanks to the team at Wiley for their input and assistance through every stage of this process, especially Stacy Kennedy and Corbin Collins.

Publisher's Acknowledgments

Acquisitions Editor: Stacy Kennedy

Editor: Corbin Collins

Contributor: Daniel Mersey

Production Editor: Tamilmani Varadharaj

Cover Image: ©3DDock/Shutterstock

Apple & Mac

iPad For Dummies, 6th Edition
978-1-118-72306-7

iPhone For Dummies, 7th Edition
978-1-118-69083-3

Macs All-in-One For Dummies,
4th Edition
978-1-118-82210-4

OS X Mavericks For Dummies
978-1-118-69188-5

Blogging & Social Media

Facebook For Dummies, 5th Edition
978-1-118-63312-0

Social Media Engagement
For Dummies
978-1-118-53019-1

WordPress For Dummies,
6th Edition
978-1-118-79161-5

Business

Stock Investing For Dummies,
4th Edition
978-1-118-37678-2

Investing For Dummies, 6th Edition
978-0-470-90545-6

Personal Finance For Dummies,
7th Edition
978-1-118-11785-9

QuickBooks 2014 For Dummies
978-1-118-72005-9

Small Business Marketing Kit
For Dummies, 3rd Edition
978-1-118-31183-7

Careers

Job Interviews For Dummies,
4th Edition
978-1-118-11290-8

Job Searching with Social Media
For Dummies, 2nd Edition
978-1-118-67856-5

Personal Branding For Dummies
978-1-118-11792-7

Resumes For Dummies, 6th Edition
978-0-470-87361-8

Starting an Etsy Business
For Dummies, 2nd Edition
978-1-118-59024-9

Diet & Nutrition

Belly Fat Diet For Dummies
978-1-118-34585-6

Mediterranean Diet For Dummies
978-1-118-71525-3

Nutrition For Dummies, 5th Edition
978-0-470-93231-5

Digital Photography

Digital SLR Photography All-in-One
For Dummies, 2nd Edition
978-1-118-59082-9

Digital SLR Video & Filmmaking
For Dummies
978-1-118-36598-4

Photoshop Elements 12
For Dummies
978-1-118-72714-0

Gardening

Herb Gardening For Dummies,
2nd Edition
978-0-470-61778-6

Gardening with Free-Range
Chickens For Dummies
978-1-118-54754-0

Health

Boosting Your Immunity
For Dummies
978-1-118-40200-9

Diabetes For Dummies, 4th Edition
978-1-118-29447-5

Living Paleo For Dummies
978-1-118-29405-5

Big Data

Big Data For Dummies
978-1-118-50422-2

Data Visualization For Dummies
978-1-118-50289-1

Hadoop For Dummies
978-1-118-60755-8

Language & Foreign Language

500 Spanish Verbs For Dummies
978-1-118-02382-2

English Grammar For Dummies,
2nd Edition
978-0-470-54664-2

French All-in-One For Dummies
978-1-118-22815-9

German Essentials For Dummies
978-1-118-18422-6

Italian For Dummies, 2nd Edition
978-1-118-00465-4

Math & Science

Algebra I For Dummies, 2nd Edition
978-0-470-55964-2

Available in print and e-book formats.

Available wherever books are sold.

For more information or to order direct visit www.dummies.com

Anatomy and Physiology
For Dummies, 2nd Edition
978-0-470-92326-9

Astronomy For Dummies,
3rd Edition
978-1-118-37697-3

Biology For Dummies, 2nd Edition
978-0-470-59875-7

Chemistry For Dummies,
2nd Edition
978-1-118-00730-3

1001 Algebra II Practice Problems
For Dummies
978-1-118-44662-1

Microsoft Office

Excel 2013 For Dummies
978-1-118-51012-4

Office 2013 All-in-One
For Dummies
978-1-118-51636-2

PowerPoint 2013 For Dummies
978-1-118-50253-2

Word 2013 For Dummies
978-1-118-49123-2

Music

Blues Harmonica For Dummies
978-1-118-25269-7

Guitar For Dummies, 3rd Edition
978-1-118-11554-1

iPod & iTunes For Dummies,
10th Edition
978-1-118-50864-0

Programming

Beginning Programming with C
For Dummies
978-1-118-73763-7

Excel VBA Programming
For Dummies, 3rd Edition
978-1-118-49037-2

Java For Dummies, 6th Edition
978-1-118-40780-6

Religion & Inspiration

The Bible For Dummies
978-0-7645-5296-0

Buddhism For Dummies,
2nd Edition
978-1-118-02379-2

Catholicism For Dummies,
2nd Edition
978-1-118-07778-8

Self-Help & Relationships

Beating Sugar Addiction
For Dummies
978-1-118-54645-1

Meditation For Dummies,
3rd Edition
978-1-118-29144-3

Seniors

Laptops For Seniors For Dummies,
3rd Edition
978-1-118-71105-7

Computers For Seniors
For Dummies, 3rd Edition
978-1-118-11553-4

iPad For Seniors For Dummies,
6th Edition
978-1-118-72826-0

Social Security For Dummies
978-1-118-20573-0

Smartphones & Tablets

Android Phones For Dummies,
2nd Edition
978-1-118-72030-1

Nexus Tablets For Dummies
978-1-118-77243-0

Samsung Galaxy S 4 For Dummies
978-1-118-64222-1

Samsung Galaxy Tabs For Dummies
978-1-118-77294-2

Test Prep

ACT For Dummies, 5th Edition
978-1-118-01259-8

ASVAB For Dummies, 3rd Edition
978-0-470-63760-9

GRE For Dummies, 7th Edition
978-0-470-88921-3

Officer Candidate Tests
For Dummies
978-0-470-59876-4

Physician's Assistant Exam
For Dummies
978-1-118-11556-5

Series 7 Exam For Dummies
978-0-470-09932-2

Windows 8

Windows 8.1 All-in-One
For Dummies
978-1-118-82087-2

Windows 8.1 For Dummies
978-1-118-82121-3

Windows 8.1 For Dummies, Book +
DVD Bundle
978-1-118-82107-7

Available in print and e-book formats.

Available wherever books are sold.

For more information or to order direct visit www.dummies.com

Printed in the USA
K060524SCI080417   01S29053000000002117